Practical Approach to Prevention and Detection of Fraud

Guidebook for internal control professionals

Practical Approach
to Prevention and Detection of Fraud

Guidebook for internal control professionals

by CK Cho, Barrister LLB (Hons.) London CFE,

Dr Charles Lau, DBA CA CIA CISA CFE

Edited by Matthew Seligman

South Eastern Publishers
2012

South Eastern Publishers Inc,

New York • Washington D.C. • London • Moscow • Hong Kong • New Delhi

228 Park Ave South,

New York, NY 10003-1502 USA

For more information e-mail info@sepublishers.com

or visit our website www.SEpublishers.com

Book design by B.B.Opastny

Printed in United States of America

First Edition: November 2012

ISBN 978-1-936531-02-8 (Paperback Edition)

ISBN 978-1-936531-03-5 (Kindle Edition)

ISBN 978-1-936531-04-2 (iBook Edition)

Library of Congress Control Number: 2012953247

This Guide Book was written to help you to:

Consider various international best practices for internal control and fraud risk management;

Outline the legal elements of fraud offences such as Theft, Deception, Fraud and Conspiracy to Defraud;

Explain the law, evidence and procedures relating to the prevention, detection and investigation of fraud;

Consider the practical and legal issues in conducting an independent internal investigation into fraudulent activities at the workplace;

Apply basic investigative skills such as interview techniques;

Set out the essential steps of a fraud investigation, including collection and preservation of evidence.

The Guide is prepared by respected professionals with extensive experience practicing and teaching fraud investigation and internal control. While the Guide is based on current Hong Kong law, it can be a useful reference book for anyone with a professional interest in fraud prevention and detection.

About the Authors

Mr. C.K. CHO 曹志光 大律師

Barrister, LLB (Hons.) London CFE DMS FCMI MIMC, MIoD

Email: ckcho@ckcho.com.hk

Mr. Cho was a senior member of the Hong Kong Independent Commission Against Corruption, where he investigated corruption, fraud, and related offences as a Chief Investigator and then as Head of the Legal Research and Management Services Unit Operations Department.

Mr. Cho is a former President of the Association of Certified Fraud Examiners, Hong Kong, a position he held from 2007 to 2008.

Mr. Cho lectures in business law, criminal law, evidence and procedures. As a consultant he provides advice on legal compliance, fraud risk management and litigation support in connection with fraud and corruption proceedings.

Dr. Charles LAU 劉健成 博士

DBA CA CIA CISA CFE

Email: kscharles@gmail.com

Dr. Lau is a Vice President of the Canadian General Accountants of Hong Kong. He is a Chartered Accountant with over 20 years' experience in internal control, auditing and internal investigation and currently works as a senior executive of a blue chip conglomerate in Hong Kong.

About the Chief Editor

Matthew Seligman

Barrister

Matthew was called to the bar at Middle Temple in October 1994 and entered practice as a tenant at 39 Essex Street the following year, where he remained until 2005.

Matthew's core experience is in all areas of Mental Health Law. He has regularly appeared for patients before Tribunals, the County Court and the High Court in Judicial Review Proceedings. His appearances in the Court of Appeal include S and Munjaz in 2003, which established the status of the Mental Health Act Code of Practice in the context of the seclusion of patients, and Re AL in 2004, which dealt with the lawfulness of the Home Secretary's re-call of a conditionally discharged patient.

Matthew has also represented parties in nearest relative displacement proceedings in the County Court and the Official Solicitor in best interests proceedings in the Family Division. Beyond these areas, Matthew advises generally on Public Law and Human Rights issues arising within the social care field and related areas.

Matthew also has extensive experience in damages claims, primarily in the field of Personal Injury and Health and Safety Law. He represented the crew of the Marchioness in Lord Justice Clarke's Wreck Inquiry in 2000 and was involved in bringing the radon gas tin miners claim in Cornwall, which were successfully compromised in late 2007. He also specialises in damages claims within a public law context, and so far in 2011 has successfully compromised five-figure claims for negligence in care, the unlawful detention of an asylum-seeking minor, and wrongful disclosure in adoption proceedings contrary to s13 of the Data Protection Act 1998.

His publications include: "Second Edition of Vincent Nelson QC's the Law of Entertainment and Broadcasting" (Sweet & Maxwell, 2000), "Lord Steyn's Lament" Psychiatry Intensive Care Journal (2007)

Acknowledgement

We want to thank all those who encouraged and supported us in this project. In particular, we wish to express our appreciation for the assistance provided by the following individuals:

Miss Winnie Kan FCCA, CPA, CIA, CISA, CFE, MBA, LLB, Editor Chapter 1

Mr. Leon Hill J.D. - Editor Chapter 2 to Chapter 9

Mr. Andrew Sloane - Editor Chapter 2 to Chapter 9

Mr. Edo de Vries Robbé

Mr. Geoff Bullen

Miss Wendy LO Wing Yee (盧詠怡)

Mr. Mark Fu Yong Qiang (付永强)

Mr. Raymond Lo (羅樹源)

Miss Karen Huang Yuzhe (黃煜喆)

The Chapter 1 of this publication was written by Dr. Charles Lau (CA, CISA, CFE) and edited by Winnie Kan FCCA, CPA, CIA, CISA, CFE, MBA, LLB.

Chapters 2-9 of this publication were written by Mr. C.K. Cho, Barrister at Law, LLB (Hons), London, CSI, CFE, DMS, FCMI, MIMC, MIoD.

Table of Contents

Chapter 1 – Internal control, enterprise risk management and good corporate governance and its practical impact upon fraud risk management

Effective internal control cannot solve all corporate problems, but defective internal controls may lead to serious corporate problems.
– Sir Cadbury

The impact of fraud

What is a fraud? Fraud exists in everyone's life. Generally, it refers to a material loss caused by deception. Frauds within corporations committed by office workers are called "white-collar" frauds. PricewaterhouseCoopers (2004) defines fraud as a broad concept that refers generally to any intentional act committed to secure an unfair or unlawful gain[1].

The Institute of Internal Auditors gives a more comprehensive definition of fraud: any illegal act characterized by deceit, concealment, or violation of trust. These acts are not dependent upon the threat of violence or physical force. Frauds are perpetrated by people and organizations to obtain money, property or services; to avoid payment or loss of services, or to secure personal business advantage (IIA, 2009)[2].

Auditors, both internal and external, are professionals on the frontline fighting with frauds. Many corporations do not have a specific fraud prevention and investigation unit, and rely on their auditors to promote fraud risk management systems, identify fraud indicators, and recommend ways to prevent fraud. However, auditors, financial auditors in particular, generally only focus on fraud that could have a material effect on their retaining firms' financial statements. Some fraud risks have no immediate financial statement impact, and these risks may not receive timely attention during routine audit reviews by corporate auditors. Anyone interested in preventing fraud should not rely upon anti-fraud programmes designed only to ensure true and fair financial statements. These fail to meet the wide range of fraud risks.

---

1   PricewaterCoopers(2004), Antifraud Programs and Controls in the Retail and Consumer Sector, (www.pwc.com)

2   IIA (2009), International Professional Practices Framework, The Institute of Internal Auditors, USA.

Traditionally, CEOs have considered fraud prevention to be the responsibility of accountants and internal auditors. When frauds were revealed, the CEOs would first curse their accountant or internal auditor, "Where have you been? Why didn't you spot this? Aren't you people supposed to protect us from fraud? If not, what are you doing to earn your salary?"

Accountants, internal auditors and others in positions responsible for internal controls and risk management start looking for other employment when a major fraud happened at their company. For the board of directors of a company, fraud not only causes financial loss, it also causes embarrassment and damage to the firm's brand and reputation. Sometimes, the fraud may be a matter of corporate life and death, as in the trader's fraud at Barings P.L.C., where just one fraud led to the collapse of a one hundred-year-old firm.

Modern fraud prevention professionals take more open-minded and proactive approaches toward tackling the problem. Prevention is always better than detection, and internal control is the most effective way to set defence against fraud, both internally and externally.

What is internal control?

Internal control is frequently mistaken for accounting control, the checks performed by accounting staff to ensure correct payments are made to the right suppliers.

In fact, internal control is much more than that. Internal control is a procedure or protocol, accounting related or not, established by management to ensure the smooth running of the business. This applies to both profit-making and not-for-profit business entities.

The IIA (2009), the authoritative professional organisationin the field of internal control, risk management and governance, gives a similar definition of control as being, "…any action taken by management, the board, and other parties to manage risk and increase the likelihood that established objectives and goals will be achieved…".

What makes for smooth running (efficient and effective operations) of a business? Smooth running can mean doing the right things at the lowest cost (effectiveness combined with efficiency) in order to meet company goals. What if while this takes place, company assets are being misappropriated? This can compromise the company's ability to achieve its objectives. An effective internal control system will help to provide reasonable assurance that:

1. operations are effectively and efficiently conducted;

2. relevant laws and regulations, and internal policies are adhered to; and,
3. company financial and management information is reliable, enabling informed decision making.

Why is internal control so important?

There are a number of factors that make internal control become a concern for the board of directors and management of a business, including -

1. The requirements of statutory law (ref. www.legislation.gov.hk)

Business organizations in Hong Kong are regulated by a number of laws, namely:
- the Companies Ordinance, such as s.59, where companies are required to maintain proper books and records as necessary to ensure a true and fair view of the state of the company's affairs and to explain its transactions;
- the Prevention of Bribery Ordinance;
- the Securities and Futures Ordinance (for listed corporations), such as s.291 regarding insider dealing;
- the Inland Revenue Ordinance;
- the Organized and Serious Crime Ordinance, such as s.25 regarding the disclosure of knowledge, or suspicion of potential money laundry transactions;
- the Theft Ordinance; and
- the Employment Ordinance.

2. The law of tort

This is part of the common law and is a fairly complicated subject. Here we only need to understand how tort law may influence internal control practices. This occurs through the fiduciary duty company directors owe to the company and its shareholders. Fiduciary duty is generally concerned with the legal obligation of an agent to act in the best interest of his principal.

3. Listing Rules

The Stock Exchange of Hong Kong Limited ("HKSE") published the Code on Corporate Governance Practices in November 2004, which was subsequently incorporated into Appendix 14 of the Main Board Listing Rules. It governs Main Board Listing Companies and specifically requires the board to ensure that the issuer maintains sound and effective internal controls to safeguard shareholders' investments and the issuer's assets (C.2). It also requires the board of directors to review the effectiveness of the system of internal control at least annually and to file a corporate governance report (C.2.1).

4. Professional bodies

Control-related professional institutions (such as the Hong Kong Institute of Certified Public Accountants "HKICPA", and the Chartered Accountants' institutes) issue pronouncements that influence internal controls practices. Examples include the Internal Control Framework issued by the HKICPA[3] and the Internal Control Framework, and Enterprise Risk Management issued by the U.S. based Committee of the Sponsoring Organizations of the Treadway Commission (COSO).

5.   The quality control of management process

Internal control is a part of management process. Management process involves five elements, namely - (1) planning, (2) organizing, (3) staffing, (4) directing, and (5) controlling.

(1) Planning

Planning sets out what is going to be done in the future, from short term/ immediate planning (covering the next 1 to 2 years), through mid-range and long term planning (3 to 5 years and beyond), and can include:

- Setting objectives and goals;
- Defining strategies to meet objectives;
- Formulating principles, policies, and procedures;
- Adhering to rules & standards;
- Formulating programmes;
- Preparing budgets; and,
- Making decisions.

(2) Organizing

Organizing establishes a structure to help achieve organizational goals, and requires an effective delegation of authority. Organizing should produce:

- A clear statement of responsibilities; and,
- A clear understanding of the types of decisions that can be made.

(3) Staffing

This involves selecting the best persons to fill positions in an organization, and includes a number of processes:

- Human resources planning;
- Recruitment; and
- Compensation.

(4) Directing

This is the process of inducing members of the organisations to perform their roles successfully. 2 components are commonly involved:

- Communicating organisational goals and transferring them into key

---

3   Internal Control and Risk Management-A Basic Framework, HKICPA.

performance indicators; and,

- Motivating staff to help achieve these goals.

(5) Controlling

This compares actual performance with predetermined standards, plans, or objectives (such as comparing monthly sales performance with the monthly sales forecast). Control is essential to ensure that corporate objectives are met. It includes these essential steps:

a) Identifying objectives and related risks (e.g. setting market share targets for each business unit);

b) Establishing standards and targets for the operating staff (e.g. the sales target for the upcoming year);

c) Measuring performance (e.g. setting up systems and procedures to track sales data and making timely sales reports);

d) Comparing performance with standards (e.g. comparing actual sales with sales budget);

e) Evaluating deviation (e.g. analysing and identifying causes for being over or under budget);

f) Correcting deviation (e.g. implementing corrective actions to ensure target achievement); and

g) Following up on corrective actions (e.g. conducting reviews to evaluate effectiveness of corrective actions).

Purpose of internal control

Primary purpose:

- to enable directors to drive their companies forward with confidence, at an appropriate speed and direction, in both good and bad times.

Secondary purpose:

- to safeguard resources and ensure the adequacy of records and accountability systems.

For a control procedure to be adequate, it must:

1. match the organisation pattern;
2. focus on critical points so that managers can devote their attention to these areas;
3. be flexible to accommodate changing plans; and
4. be economical and cost-effective.

Principles of internal control

- Internal control is a process. It is a means to an end, not an end itself.
- Control is effected by people throughout the organization, including the board of directors, management, and other staff, and is geared towards the achievement of objectives.
- Control requires commitment and support of staff (at all levels); it will not succeed just by decree from the top.
- Those who manage operations must be accountable for the controls over their operations.
- Organisations are constantly interacting and adapting. Controls must be responsive to changes within the organization, and in the external environment. As risks change, so will controls.
- Effective control demands that a balance be maintained between autonomy and integration and that a moderate course be set between maintaining the status quo and adapting to change.
- The more clearly defined objectives of the organisation are, the better will be the chances of achieving effective control.
- Control can never provide absolute assurance, only reasonable assurance. This is because of the inherent limitations of internal control:
    - Internal control cannot rectify wrong decisions made by top management;
    - Human errors are inevitable;
    - Collusive circumvention of controls is always possible;
    - Management level overrides of key controls is always possible; and,
    - Cost-benefit analysis may stall the implementation of controls when the potential benefits do not appear justified.
- Internal control is only a part of the management process. Effective internal controls are not a remedy for poor decisions, ineffective management, or unpredictable external events.

To conclude:

Good management and effective internal controls can help to ensure that an organisation is in a position to deal quickly and positively with adverse circumstances. They can also help to limit the worst effects.

Categories of control

Based on the nature of the control processes, internal control processes can be classified as:

1.   Preventive Control

This type of control helps to discourage the occurrence of undesirable events.

E.g. all the purchase requisitions over certain amount must have prior approval of the CEO;

2.   Detective Control

These measures detect and correct undesirable events.
E.g. Bank Reconciliation;

3.   Directive Control

These are actions taken to cause or encourage a desirable event to occur.
E.g. Policy & Procedures; and,

4.   Mitigating (compensating) Control

This refers to other actions (control steps) that can serve to mitigate the risks associating with certain processes or transactions when other controls are absent or too costly relative to their benefits.
E.g. supervisory review (over the monthly sales report).

Preventive and direct controls are better than detective controls. Compensating control is acceptable as long as it is economical to implement.

Models of Internal Control

Internal control frameworks are designed to provide insight into the structure and working of control, and to provide a fresh look at the assessment of control.

Popular frameworks include:

(a)   COSO Model of USA

The Internal Control – Integrated Framework published by the Committee of Sponsoring Organizations of the Treadway Commission (COSO[4]) in 1992, defines internal control as a process effected by an organization's board of directors, management and other personnel, designed to provide reasonable assurance regarding the achievement of objectives in three categories:

- Effectiveness and efficiency of operations;
- Reliability of reporting; and,
- Compliance with applicable rules, laws and regulations.

The COSO Model treats internal control as a process:

---

4   COSO - Committee of Sponsoring Organizations of the Treadway Commission - is a private sector initiative. It was originally formed in 1985 and was jointly sponsored by five major financial professional associations in the United States.

Chart 1 – Internal control process

| Define Objectives | → | Access Risks | → | Evaluate Controls |

Chart 2 – Key components of COSO

Components	Key Concerns
Control Environment	• *"Integrity can't be compromised" communicated to staff?* • *Control- conscious throughout the organization?* • *Authority and responsibility well-defined?* • *Right level of attention from the board?*
Risk Assessment	• *Entity-wide objectives linked to activity-level?* • *Significant internal and external risks identified and assessed?* • *Critical changes identified?* • *Policies and procedures modified in response to identified changes?*
Control Activities	• *Appropriate control activities for the operations?* • *Control activities in place to ensure the adherence to policies and procedures?*
Information and Communication	• *Pertinent information (financial/non-financial) identified, captured and communicated to relevant personnel?* • *Clear expectations communicated to staff (downward communication)?* • *Clear reports and other feedback to management (upward communication)?* • *Effective communication across the entity and with other parties?*
Monitoring	• *Measures in place to evaluate the control functions?* • *Deficiencies reported to the right people?* • *Policies and procedures modified?*

The framework set out in Chart 3 applies to all activities and subsidiaries of a listed company.

Chart 3 Coso Framework

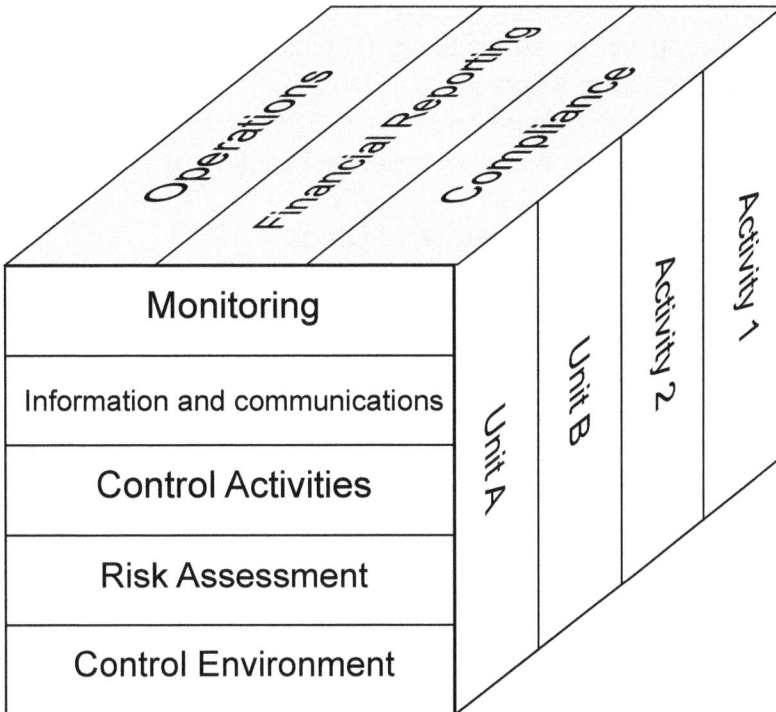

(Adopted from: HKICPA (2005), Internal Control and Risk Management – A Basic Framework)

(b)   CoCo Model of Canada

The CoCo Model was developed by the Criteria of Control Board of the Canadian Institute of Chartered Accountants in 1995. CoCo focuses on behavioural values rather than control structure procedures as the fundamental basis for internal control. It uses four essential elements as groupings within which it articulates 20 criteria for control, structured in four main categories: purpose, commitment, capability, and monitoring and learning criteria.

(c)   The Cadbury Committee Report of UK

The Cadbury Report[5] states that for directors to meet their responsibilities for maintaining adequate accounting records, they need to maintain a system of internal control over the financial management of the company that includes procedures designed to minimize the risk of fraud.

---

5   Report of the Committee on the Financial Aspects of Corporate Governance, UK, December 1992.

(d)   The Internal Control and Risk Management – A Basic Framework of Hong Kong

This is a guide issued by the Hong Kong Institute of Certified Public Accountants at the invitation of the Hong Kong Stock Exchange "HKSE". It adopts the definition and conceptual framework described in the COSO report to help listed companies cope with the Code on Corporate Governance Practice as issued by HKSE.

(e)   The Control Framework of China

The Basic Standard for Enterprise Internal Control, (企业内部控制基本规范, *the Standard*), was jointly issued in June 2008 by the Chinese Ministry of Finance (财政部), the National Audit Office (审计署), and three major industry regulators including the China Securities Regulatory Commission (证监会), the China Banking Regulatory Commission (银监会),and the China Insurance Regulatory Commission (保监会). It governs all listed companies in PRC. Under the Standard, internal control was defined with the same five elements as the 1992 COSO Internal Control Model.

Preventing and Detecting Fraud - Whose Responsibility?

It is "common sense" to assume that internal or external auditors are checking the books to prevent and detect fraud. We expect auditors to alert management when they find a fraud loophole, or when a fraud has been detected.

Managing fraud risks effectively and efficiently requires the combined efforts of all concerned parties in an organization. The following paragraphs set out the roles of executives for various functional duties fighting fraud. These are for general reference only. Each organization's unique situation will warrant a customized division of duties.

(i) The board of directors

- The Board is ultimately responsible for the prevention and detection of fraud. Specifically, the Board should establish fraud prevention strategies and policies, delegate appropriate staff to implement the strategies, periodically review the organization's risk management and internal control systems, and, when a fraud is revealed, take appropriate action to rectify the situation.

- The Code on Corporate Governance Practice requires the board of directors of listed corporations of Hong Kong to review their internal control systems at least once a year. The Code also recommends disclosure of additional information regarding risk management processes and internal control systems.

(ii) The Chief Financial Officer (CFO)

- The CFO should advise the Board on the formulation of fraud prevention strategies.

- Another very important role of a CFO is to guide operations management in the design, implementation, and self-review of internal control and risk management systems.

(iii) Operating management (general managers, and supervisors of business units and functions)

- These managers occupy a frontline position preventing and detecting fraud activities within their areas of supervision.

- They should design and implement procedures and systems for the reporting of fraudulent activities and irregularities.

- When any suspicious fraudulent irregularities have been noted, they should be reported to the appropriate level of management, as identified in the company's published fraud prevention strategies and policies, issued by the Board of Directors.

(iv) Internal / external auditors

- Auditors are neither legally nor primarily responsible for the prevention and detection of fraud. The Kingston Cotton Mills case (1896) stated that an auditor is a watchdog, not a bloodhound. However, if there is anything calculated to excite reasonable suspicion, he should probe it to the bottom; but in the absence of anything of that kind he is only bound to be reasonably cautious and careful.

- Under this analogy, the "watchdog" (auditor) is expected to growl or bark when an "intruder" (i.e. weaknesses of internal control) is suspected or detected. When a suspicious transaction is detected by the auditors during an audit (i.e. indicators of fraud), the "bloodhounds" (professional investigators or forensic accountants) should then be called in.

- The Hong Kong Standard on Auditing 240 requires auditors to maintain professional skepticism throughout the audit, recognizing the possibility that a material misstatement due to fraud could exist, notwithstanding the auditor's past experience of the honesty and integrity of the entity management and those charged with governance.

- The auditor, and in particular the internal auditor, should be responsible for both identifying material internal control weaknesses that provide opportunities for fraudulent penetration and for spotting indicators of potential fraud. When those indicators of fraud are noted, the internal auditors should immediately summon management's attention and suggest whether forensic investigators should be called in.

- The Institute of Internal Auditors states that internal auditors should evaluate internal controls' effectiveness and efficiency and promote continuous improvement focusing on:
  - Reliability and integrity of financial and operational information;
  - Effectiveness and efficiency of operations;
  - Safeguarding of assets; and
  - Compliance with laws, regulations, and contracts.

(v) Anti-fraud / corporate security officer (where applicable)

For large corporations, it is appropriate to have a designated senior officer to combat fraud tasked with the following responsibilities:

- Assisting the corporation to draft an appropriate statement of fraud strategies and policies;
- Implementing fraud strategies, policies, and fraud response plans;
- Initiating and overseeing all fraud investigations and conducting follow-up actions accordingly;
- Receiving and evaluating confidential enquiries from staff regarding fraudulent activities, and confidentially advising enquirers independently; and
- Reporting suspected cases of fraud to appropriate levels of management. For example, if he suspects that his supervisor is a suspect, he should report to a more senior level of management or to an independent non-executive director, such as the chair of audit committee.

(vi) Human resources manager

- His primary responsibility is to ensure fair and effective internal disciplinary procedures for suspects of fraudulent activities; and
- He should give advice on the development of a fraud response plan, in particular with regards to compliance with employment legislation and regulations, human rights protections, and similar laws.

(vii)   Audit committee

- The Listing Rules of Hong Kong Stock Exchange require audit committees to conduct annual review of their companies' risk management and internal control systems, and to make any necessary disclosures in their corporations' governance reports. This includes review of the design and implementation of anti-fraud programmes and controls.

- In particular, the audit committee should monitor the integrity of financial statements, and assess the corporation's performance in the prevention of fraud that might lead to distortions in the financial statements.

- Some audit committees require that a corporation should institute a whistle-blowing system, an arrangement which enables employees and other stakeholders to confidentially raise concerns about irregularities directly to the audit committees.

- The audit committee should ensure the corporation has proper policies and procedures in place to ensure independent investigations of suspected fraud cases and follow-up action.

- The audit committee is also responsible for reviewing and assessing the effectiveness of both the internal and external audit activities, including the identification of fraud indicators.

Fraud risk management strategies

A corporation usually has strategies for business; it should also implement strategies for fraud prevention. Fraud strategies address fraud risks identified and assessed by management.

There are four generic fraud risk management strategies:

i) Risk avoidance

Do not engage in businesses that would present these risks. For example, if you do not want to risk cash loss, you can avoid selling goods for cash, and insist that settlement should be made by cheques.

ii) Risk retention

You may choose to accept risks because they are considered "small" and relatively inconsequential. For example, if there is an inventory shrinkage of 0.05% every year and your firm finds that this is acceptable, it may choose to accept the loss. The decision depends on the firm's risk appetite. Risk appetite is the level of risk that the firm is willing to accept, and this is usually determined by the board of directors. Risk appetite may vary over time, particularly in time of recession. In a country with high compliance costs (i.e. serious penalties for tax law violations), management would prudently opt for lower risk tolerance of compliance matters.

iii) Risk sharing

Some risks may be controlled so that they are acceptable to the firm. For example, if the firm is involved in the betting industry, the risks of betting fraud are high. The firm should institute sufficient controls to manage this so that fraud risk losses are kept to a minimum.

iv) Risk transfer

Sometimes management will be aware of risks, and choose to transfer the risks outside the firm. For example: a staff fiduciary bond can be made to an insurance company so that the risk of loss caused by internal staff is transferred to the insurance company.

A firm usually takes a combined strategy to address its fraud risks. See the fraud risk matrix below.

Chart 4 Fraud Risk Matrix

	Low risk	Medium risk	High risk
High cost impact	Retention	Sharing	Avoidance
Medium cost impact	Retention	Sharing	Management
Low cost impact	Retention	Retention	Retention

Chosen strategies should be communicated properly to those responsible for implementation by writing, seminars, action plans, etc. Fraud strategies should be reviewed on a periodic basis to ensure they are still valid and responsive to the changing environment.

Design of internal control: fraud prevention perspective

For larger companies, the current components of the COSO framework could also apply to assessment of fraud risk for the set up of the control framework. The control activities involved would probably include fraud policies, fraud training, whistleblowing policies, and adequate internal controls.

How to work with fraud investigators

When a fraud is suspected to have occurred in his corporation, the first question that a professional internal auditor or corporate accountant should ask is whether he has the sufficient and relevant experience, skills and knowledge to respond to it. If he does not have the relevant experience, skills and knowledge regarding fraud investigation, the best choice is to refer the matter to a professional fraud investigator. It doesn't necessarily mean a total hand-off where the internal auditor would make no further contribution to the investigation. Concerned in-house personnel should actively participate in the process, utilizing their expertise accordingly. To have synergy working with fraud investigators, company personnel should:

1. <u>Know what they do best</u>

    A corporation usually delegates the investigation of suspected fraud to in-house auditors or accountants, because they are trained in auditing and internal control skills. Senior management often forgets that accounting professionals are not equipped with the necessary skills for fraud investigation. Accountants and auditors are trained to identify fraud indicators. When fraud indicators are noted, their role is to report them to the appropriate level of management for action. Auditors are watchdogs. They are not hounds. When auditors find fraud indicators, they bark, and assist in the hunting. Investigators are the hounds.

    Before referring a case to fraud investigators, internal auditors should:

()   Complete an initial assessment of the allegations.
- Consider what would happen if the allegations turn out to be false.
- Consider whether there is a possible innocent explanation.
- Ask whether there is sufficient evidence to report to law enforcement.
(ii)   Outline the importance of legal and regulatory issues.
(iii) Determine what outside support is required, including asking

<u>Should the corporation engage an outside professional fraud investigator?</u>

<u>How to find a competent fraud investigator?</u>

The auditors could participate in the investigation by contributing to:

    a) The processes and systems within the corporation

    The auditors have been working with the corporation, so they are familiar with the in-house procedures and systems, in particular how to trace the accountabilities and process records of suspicious transactions. Their work will help the external fraud investigators undertake the internal process and trace the targets.

b) Preservation of evidence

When the auditors have identified indicators of fraud, they are at the front line of the fraud investigation, and they should preserve any evidence they have collected. In particular, they should take over physical evidence before the suspect(s) can remove or destroy it. This control process should be done before interviews are conducted. At this stage, fraud investigators should be consulted if they have been engaged, and auditors should take necessary steps to not alert the suspect(s).

Evidence may be classified as: (1) Physical evidence; (2) Electronic evidence; (3) Testimonial evidence from witnesses and suspects.

The auditors should properly record any evidence from the outset, including accurate notes of when, how, where, and from whom the evidence was obtained. It is also important that written consent should be obtained from the appropriate business heads before removing any items.

c)   Coordination between top management and fraud investigators

Internal auditors are the appropriate liaison to facilitate fraud investigators in the course of their investigation. For example, internal auditors can explain in detail the key transaction processes and document trails related to the investigation. They can also coordinate with business unit heads and human resources managers regarding the suspect(s)' background.

2.   Know the fraud investigators

Fraud investigators may be public officers (such as police officers, or investigators of the Hong Kong Independent Commission Against Corruption,) or professional private consultants. In the case of private consultants, it is important to know the investigator's background, qualifications, experience and reputation. Professional consultants operating in this role would not hesitate to provide a potential client with their details and references.

3.   How the partnership works

In-house auditors should need to have an understanding of the investigation process. Consider this sample investigation programme diagram as reference -

Chart 5 Steps to Investigate a Fraud

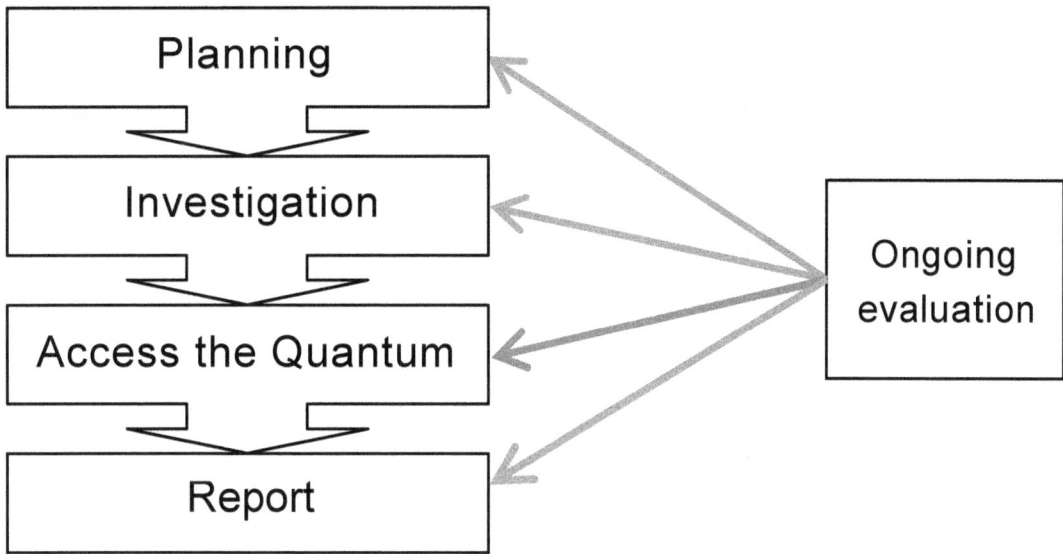

| Planning |
| Investigation |
| Access the Quantum |
| Report |

Ongoing evaluation

Planning the Investigation

Each fraud investigation should be approached as if it would result in litigation, and it aims to:

- Identify logical and reasonable alternatives for identifiable issues;
- Identify source of documentation and information;
- Determine the issues for financial analysis; and,
- Consider the roles and needs of the end-users of the results of the investigation. They will likely be the Board of directors, the Chair of the audit committee, external auditors, the CEO, other corporate management, legal counsel and the head of human resources.

Key Steps of Planning an Investigation

- Review and assess the available evidence.
- Develop a preliminary hypothesis. This is what you initially believed to have happened based **on a series of assumptions.** The preliminary hypothesis should include alternative explanations for the alleged events. The investigator should remain open to alternative explanations throughout the investigation.
- Outline the series of assumptions identified. For example:
  - Who might be involved?
  - What might have happened?
  - Why might the allegation be true?
  - Where are the possible concealment places or methods?
  - When did the fraud take place (past, present, or future)?

- How is the fraud being perpetrated?
- During the investigation the assumptions are then tested to determine if they are accurate and provable.
- Review and assess the available evidence. Determine where the evidence is likely to be in order to test the assumptions (i.e. the source of the evidence). The sources may include interviews, background research, accounting records, direct and circumstantial evidence.
- Determine what evidence is necessary to prove fraud.
- Decide the best investigative approach
  - Interviews - Who? What questions? When?
  - Background research on the suspect(s)

Chart 6 Key steps of planning an investigation

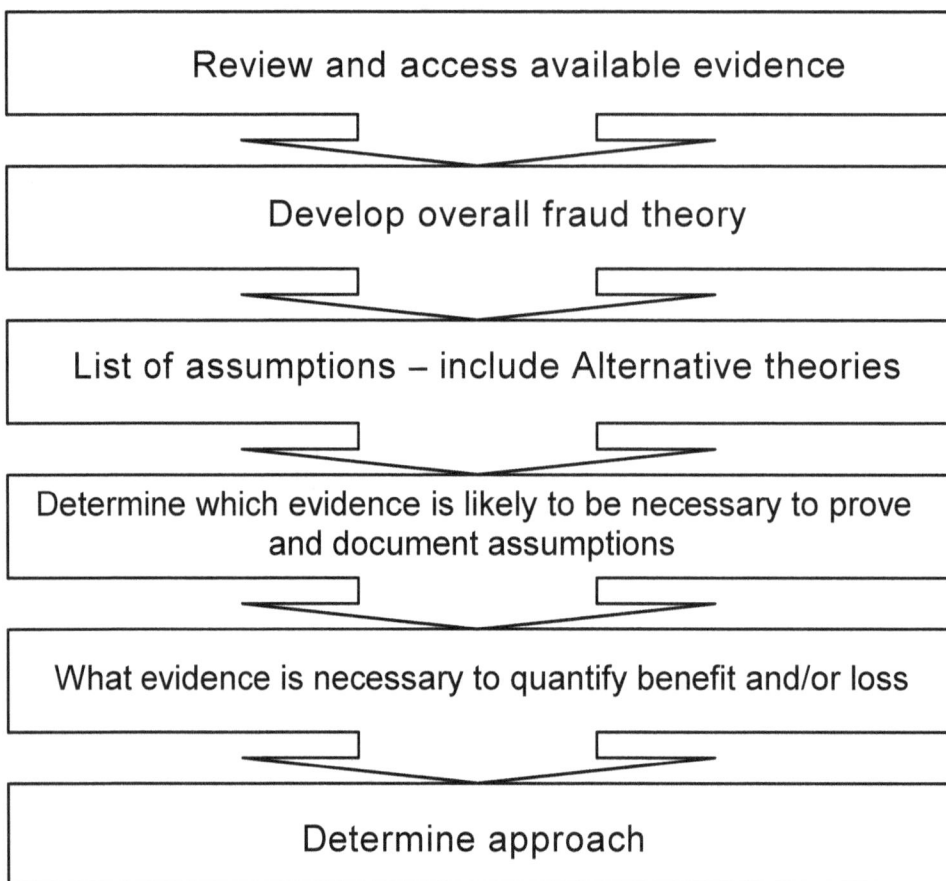

Review and access available evidence

Develop overall fraud theory

List of assumptions – include Alternative theories

Determine which evidence is likely to be necessary to prove and document assumptions

What evidence is necessary to quantify benefit and/or loss

Determine approach

The preliminary hypothesis should be constantly refined and amended as each step of the investigation is completed. It may be necessary to completely redesign the hypothesis or expand the hypothesis to include other individuals or other fraud committed by the same suspect. This may result in a revision of the plan and approach.

During the investigation, the investigator should constantly evaluate and review:

- The suspect's sphere of influence
- The areas of influence - should you consider investigating other areas?
- The pattern of conduct - how did the suspect commit and cover up the fraud?
- The relationship between employees and systems to ensure that all possible frauds are being detected.

The Interview Process and Note Taking

An interview is a question-and-answer session designed to elicit information. Generally an interview can be held:

- during the initial stages of the investigation to collect evidence for the investigation; and,
- at the end of an investigation to confirm the investigator's conclusions and to determine what the witness knows.

A trained, experienced investigator should be consulted before attempting an interview.

An internal auditor's role may involve preparation for a witness interview. In addition to preparing an outline to be used for the interview, the investigator may request that the internal auditor attend the interview and assist in note-taking.

Taking notes is an extremely important role. Do not try and write down all the information. Instead concentrate on key words that will assist you in reproducing detailed notes immediately after the interview. MAKE SURE YOU MAKE DETAILED NOTES as soon as possible.

If the witness states something that is key to your investigation, it is best to write it down verbatim. Enclose the statement in quotes to indicate a verbatim statement. In addition to recording what the witness has said, you should document the circumstances of the interview (i.e. date, time, location and those in attendance) along with the behaviour of the witness.

Assembling and Examining Documents

The investigation team reviews the information provided to ensure it is accurate and complete. After all of the documentary evidence is collected the investigators must review and interpret the integrity and relevance of the available documentation. The evidence must be assessed to determine if it is sufficient to prove the fraud.

Tips on handling documents in a fraud investigation

- Obtain originals where feasible (the best evidence rule). Make 2 copies at once; 1 clean copy and 1 to be used as a working copy.
- Do not touch originals any more than necessary; they may later need to undergo forensic analysis, such as fingerprinting, and handwriting analysis. If possible, do not remove staples from originally stapled documents.
- When making a copy, ensure the document is completely copied including notes attached and writing on the back of any pages.

Assess the Quantum

- Based on the evidence collected and checked by the investigators, the amount of fraud activities involved may be identified.

Report

- A report is the formal means by which findings, conclusions and opinions of the fraud auditor are expressed and documented.
- Before preparing a report, first consider the user of the report. Define your objectives. In most cases a report will be used to support the investigator's expert testimony in court.
- The objective is to provide the user with the evidence to prove the alternately legal element of the offences or to support claims for civil remedies. It is ultimately up to the court to determine, on the available evidence as to whether a fraud has been proved or whether or not damages have been incurred as a result of fraud.
- A well-drafted report typically uses a structure which mirrors how evidence would be presented by an expert witness. Typically the report will have the following features:
  - Effective date of the report
  - Identity of the user
  - Purpose of the engagement
  - Summary of conclusions and opinions
  - Background information and summary of the allegations
    + Details of specific issues to be addressed in the report
  - Scope of review
    + Documents reviewed and relied upon
    + List of interviewees
  - Detailed findings will include
    + Outline of approach
    + Outline of the evidence supporting the conclusion
    + Details of the assumptions made, qualifications, and limitations
    + Disclaimer and limitations on the dissemination of the report
    + Schedules, exhibits, appendices

4.   What to do when the investigation has "closed"

When the investigation has been closed, there are three possible results: the case was substantiated, with sufficient evidence against the suspect(s); the case was not substantiated with no fraud uncovered; or, fraud was not found, but there was management malpractice, and someone accountable for this has been identified.

At this stage, the internal auditors should follow up the case, paying attention to:

(i)   Insurance considerations - if the corporation has suffered economic loss

- Review the policy. Find out the terms and conditions of the coverage.
- Note the time frames for notice and delivery of the Proof of Loss. In general, the client should contact his insurance company as soon as possible. If not, he may lose protection.
- Mitigation - he is obliged to take steps to mitigate his losses.

(ii)   Considerations related to the suspect(s)

- Dismiss employee with cause, avoiding publicity?
- Civil recovery. Are damages recoverable?
- Criminal proceedings - put suspect in jail?
- Recover under fidelity bond policy?

(iii)   Future prevention – learning from mistakes

- What improvements need to be made in order to avoid similar fraud in the future?

Appendix 1 to this chapter is a list of anti-fraud and Regulatory Bodies, Regulatory, Supervisory and Investigative Organisations and their Activities.

Appendix 1 – Anti-Fraud and Regulatory Bodies, Regulatory, Supervisory and Investigative Organisations and their Activities

Transparency International

> A non-governmental organisation dedicated to increasing government accountability and curbing both international and national corruption.

World Bank Institute Governance Group

> The Governance group of the World Bank Institute (WBI) facilitates action-oriented and participatory programmes to promote good governance and curb corruption in its client countries.

OECD: Corruption

> The OECD has assumed a leading role in preventing international bribery and corruption. The website provides detailed information about its efforts.

GRECO: Group of States against Corruption

> The aim of the GRECO is to improve its members' capacity to fight corruption by monitoring the compliance of States with their undertakings in this field. It was established by the Council of Europe but membership is open to any state that meets the relevant criteria, and the United States joined it in 2000.

Combating economic and organised crime

> A Council of Europe website with information about efforts to combat corruption, cybercrime, organised crime, money laundering and trafficking in human beings.

The United Nations Office on Drugs and Crime

> The United Nations Office on Drugs and Crime (UNODC) is a global leader in the fight against illicit drugs and international crime.

UNICORN

> UNICORN is a Global Unions Anti-corruption Network which aims to mobilise and support trade unions to combat corruption. It was set up in 2001 as a joint initiative of three major international trade union bodies: The Trade Union Advisory Committee to the OECD; Public Services International; and the International Confederation of Free Trade Unions.

Stability Pact Anti-corruption Initiative

> It provides information about international efforts to combat corruption in Southeastern Europe.

UK Treasury Annual Fraud Reports

> An analysis of reported fraud in Government Departments together with anti-fraud guidance produced by the Treasury.

Fraud Advisory Panel

The Fraud Advisory Panel is an independent body of volunteers drawn from the public and private sectors in the United Kingdom. Members include representatives from the law and accountancy professions, industry associations, financial institutions, government agencies, law enforcement, regulatory authorities and academia.

Serious Organised Crime Agency

SOCA was created by the British government in April 2006. It has taken over the functions of the National Crime Squad, the National Criminal Intelligence Service, the role of HMRC in investigating drug trafficking and related criminal finance and some of the functions of the UK Immigration Service in dealing with organised immigration crime.

The Serious Fraud Office

The aim of the SFO is to investigate and prosecute serious and complex fraud and to deter fraud and maintain confidence in the probity of business and financial services in the United Kingdom.

Fraud Reduction website

This website is published by the National Working Group on Fraud on behalf of the UK Association of Chief Police Officers. The website deals primarily with commercial fraud in a policing context.

Committee on Standards in Public Life

The Committee on Standards in Public Life was set up in October, 1994. Its terms of reference are: To examine current concerns about standards of conduct of all holders of public office in the United Kingdom, including arrangements relating to financial and commercial activities, and make recommendations as to any changes in present arrangements which might be required to ensure the highest standards of propriety in public life.

British Bankers' Association (BBA)

Among its many services the BBA provides information about the prevention of fraud and money laundering.

UK Financial Services Authority

It regulates the financial services industry and has four objectives: maintaining market confidence; promoting public understanding of the financial system; protecting consumers; and fighting financial crime.

Get Safe Online

A website produced by the British Government in cooperation with HSBC, Microsoft, the Serious Organised Crime Agency and other organisations to give advice on problems ranging from computer viruses and spams to online rip-offs and identity fraud.

Home Office - Identity Theft

A website produced by the Home Office Identity Fraud Steering Committee, a collaboration between UK financial bodies, government and the police to combat the threat of identity theft.

Consumer Direct: Scams

A telephone and online consumer advice service supported by the Department of Trade and Industry United Kingdom, to advise on how to recorgnise and avoid scams.

OLAF European Anti-Fraud Office

Press releases and reports from OLAF, the European Commission's anti-fraud office.

European Court of Auditors

It describes itself as "the financial conscience of the European Union".

U.S. Securities and Exchange Commission

The SEC is an independent, nonpartisan, quasi-judicial regulatory agency with responsibility for administering the federal securities laws.

US Financial Crimes Enforcement Network (FinCEN)

FinCEN was established in 1990 by the US Treasury Department to collate, analyse, and disseminate information on financial crimes, especially drug money laundering.

Internet Crime Complaint Center

The Internet Crime Complaint Center is a partnership between the US Federal Bureau of Investigation and the National White-Collar Crime Center.

NASD Regulation Inc.

It is the independent subsidiary of the National Association of Securities Dealers, Inc. to regulate the securities industry and the Nasdaq Stock Market.

Cybercrime

The website of the Computer Crime and Intellectual Property Section of the Criminal Division of the U.S. Department of Justice.

Inter-American Convention Against Corruption

A convention adopted in March 1996 by the Organisation of American States.

RespondaNet : The Americas' Accountability/Anti-Corruption project (AAA)

The AAA is funded by the United States Agency for International Development, Bureau for Latin America and the Caribbean, and aims to support anti-corruption initiatives and to strengthen public sector financial management. It is a bilingual English/Spanish site.

Royal Canadian Mounted Police: Frauds and Scams

Information about how to recognise, report and stop frauds.

Australia Scamwatch

An official Australian government website with warnings about various types of scams.

Financial Arbiter of the Czech Republic

Contains annual reports and examples of the Arbiter's work.

Nigeria's Economic and Financial Crimes Commission

Economic and financial crimes like Advance Fee Fraud, money laundering, and corruption have had severe negative consequences on Nigeria, including decreased foreign direct investments in the country and tainting of Nigeria's national image. Recognition of the magnitude and gravity of the situation led to the establishment of the Economic and Financial Crimes Commission.

Chapter 2 – Fraud – Overview

I. Introduction

Fraud happens when a person uses deception with dishonesty to cheat6 another person out of something valuable or to gain an advantage for himself.

In Hong Kong, the law in this area has developed over the years resulting in a patchwork of provisions scattered throughout the legislation and the common law.

This book will examine and arrange all of this materialto offer a helping hand to people having a professional interest in the law and in the prevention, detection and investigation of fraud. The main focus is on the criminal law. Although footnotes are used in this chapter to give the reader entry points for further research, their use elsewhere in the book will be limited.

The challenge with fraud is to detect not only the criminal, but also the crime. This is because fraud is a concealed, hidden act. Most thefts, burglaries or robberies are obvious either when they happen or very soon afterwards. Fraud is usually discovered sometime later, if at all. This is what makes it both different and difficult to investigate and prosecute.

To work effectively in fraud detection, investigation and prevention, you need to know the components of the criminal charge. Only then can you identify the evidence needed to prove the elements of the offence in court. But what looks complicated, at first, in many cases is not. This book will guide you through the legal patchwork and provide you with an overview of fraud prevention, detection and investigation.

It is important to not let the fine distinctions in which lawyers sometimes involve themselves distract and confuse you! Non-lawyers may be uncomfortable with the idea that there can be a deception that is not dishonest. This type of distinction becomes easier to understand when considered in the context of its purpose, to channel, categorize and define the evidence required in a particular case. Understanding these parameters makes the terms easier to deal with. We will try to make the safe boundary lines clear.

---

6   The offence of fraud was originally known as "cheat"– see Litton "The Difference between a Lie and a False Pretence" from Law Lectures for Practitioners (1989 HKLJ) 77, at 81.

II. Fraud, Corruption and Bribery compared

Fraud

Fraud is often referred to as the "gentleman's theft", and is reasonably correlated with the rise in white-collar crime in recent years. There are many different kinds of this activity, and the Law Reform Commission of Hong Kong has stated that, *"the term 'fraud' is probably one of the widest in the law"*[7]. Depending on a variety of factors, fraud may be prosecuted as a crime or as a claim in civil court. You need to know which kind of fraud definition will apply to your particular case. Hong Kong's major fraud offences are listed in Chapter 4.

In this section, we will explain what common law fraud is, and how it specifically differs from bribery and corruption.

As mentioned, fraud is about the act of cheating. As courts apply this term, "cheating" must include two elements. The act must (i) be dishonest, and (ii) involve concealment or hiding of activities. This is the same with all types of fraud which, in most cases, will involve a deception of some kind.

It may surprise a non-lawyer that there is a kind of fraud where deception does not need to be proved.

A deception not proved

For example, consider that if an employee did not disclose his financial interest in a contract awarded by his employer, he has not deceived his employer – he has merely concealed his interest in the contract.

Despite the absence of any clear act of deception, the law still regards the rights of the employer as being prejudiced, because the employer should be entitled to consider the potential conflict of interest before awarding the contract.

If this employee planned with other persons to do something with an intent to defraud, prejudicing the employer's rights, their plan would be considered a conspiracy to defraud, even though the employer may have actually benefited from the contract. That this conduct could be subject to criminal prosecution may be shocking news to employees who believe they are being clever, not dishonest, but merely doing their best to maximize profits.

Not disclosing an interest in the contract could also be characterized as a false representation of having no material financial interest in the matter. This evidence

---

7   The Law Reform Commission of Hong Kong – para 2.1, p14 of their July 1996 Report on Creation of a Substantive Offence of Fraud (Topic 24).

of deception would be relevant and admissible against the employee under these circumstances.

In some cases fraud can be proved without showing deception. But evidence of deception will support a determination of criminal intent to defraud and dishonesty.

The laws relating to fraud hold many such surprises, making the task of understanding fraud a more lively one. Offering further challenge, the laws relating to fraud necessarily involve the examination of civil law principles governing property, trust, fiduciary duties of agents and directors, companies and contracts.

Corruption

Corruption can also be classified as a crime or a civil cause of action. It can occur in both public and private arenas. It happens when there is an abuse of power by a person in a position of authority or trust. Usually his objective is to either gain or give some kind of special advantage.

In most corruption cases it will not be necessary to prove dishonesty. Focus is on the abuse of power, which courts decisions have defined as using power in a way that is inconsistent with the way it should properly be used.

Frequently corruption will include deception, when an act that appears to bear official approval has not actually been used for official purposes, but it is important to note that deception is not an element of the legal definition of corruption.

Corruption also does not necessarily involve the offering, giving or receiving of a reward – see _HKSAR v Shum Kwok-sher_ [2001] 3 HKLRD 399[8]. This distinguishes corruption from bribery.

Bribery

Bribery is a specific form of corruption. It is a crime involving the offer or acceptance of any form of reward or inducement for a "corrupt purpose", as mentioned above. Bribery prevention has a key role to play in Hong Kong's anti-corruption initiatives because the central plank of the anti-corruption criminal legislation in Hong Kong is the Prevention of Bribery Ordinance (Chapter 201), 1970.

Bribery is not a civil cause of action. Anti-bribery and anti-corruption agencies recognize the concept of "secret profit" as being the most closely related principle in civil law.

---

8 "Specific corrupt acts are inherently difficult to detect let alone prove in the normal way," Attorney General v Hui Kin Hong [1995] 1 HKCLR 227.

III. Fraud – civil and criminal definitions

This is first of the many legal definitions presented in this book. The formal legal language cannot be avoided, but we will try to explain it as simply as possible. It helps to consider these definitions as "law checklists".

Civil Fraud

The leading authority on civil fraud (which used to be known as the tort of deceit) is the old United Kingdom common law decision of *Derry v Peek [1889] 14 App. Cas. 33* adopted by several modern decisions including Tugenhat J in *GE Commercial Finance Limited v Gee & Others*.

Derry v Peek provides a checklist of elements required to prove civil fraud:

LAW CHECKLIST

"The tort of deceit" involves a -

1. false representation made by the defendant;
    a)   who knows it to be untrue, or
    b)   who has no belief in its truth, or
    c)   who is reckless as to its truth.

2. if the defendant intended that the plaintiff should act in reliance on such representation; and,

3. the plaintiff in fact did so; then the defendant will be liable in deceit for

4. the damage caused.

("Tort" is not a dessert pastry, but rather a legal term of art for a wrong act redressable in civil court. "Plaintiff" and "Defendant" refer to the victim and the person accused of committing the fraud respectively.)

There are three things to particularly note about this definition:

1. It is not necessary to show that the fraudster profited, as long as it can be shown that the victim's rights were compromised or he lost money as a result of the act;

2. There must be intentional or reckless deception by the fraudster. "Recklessness" means ignoring a known, and significant, risk; and,

3. The victim must be able to show that a reasonable person under the same circumstances would have been similarly fooled.

4. There is a high standard of proof in civil fraud cases. Most civil issues are decided on a balance of probabilities (51% or greater winning the case), but fraud issues must be proved nearer to a certainty of approximately 80%.

Criminal Fraud

Fraud is a criminal offence both under statute and at common law in Hong Kong. The main criminal fraud offences each has separate and quite specific definitions which are set out in Chapter 3. They are:

- *Theft Ordinance* - the five statutory offences that violate sections 16A, 17 and 18, 18A and 18B of the Theft Ordinance may all be committed by one person acting alone or in concert with another; and,
- *Common Law* - conspiracy to defraud, where two or more persons have conspired together.

Chart 7 – Summary of Main Points of Comparison between Civil and Criminal Fraud

"Offence"	"Deception"	"Dishonesty"	Persons involved in fraud	Consequence
CIVIL				
Civil Fraud	Deception, must be intentional	n/a	1+	Loss to victim, prejudice to victim's legal rights
CRIMINAL				
Statutory Fraud - s16A, Theft Ordinance	Deception	n/a	1+	Financial/property benefit to any person other than the victim, Financial/property loss to any person other than defendant
Obtaining by Deception - s17, Theft Ordinance	Deception	Dishonesty	1+	Benefit to defendant or others
Conspiracy to Defraud, common law	n/a	Dishonesty	2+	Financial or economic loss to victim, prejudice to victim's legal or economic rights

IV. Conclusion

Fraud and corruption are chargeable in different forms and in different forums. The checklists that are provided in the following chapters detail specific offences for different cases. These checklists will identify what must be proven, enabling you to determine the evidence you will need to collect.

Q&A

1. What is an example of a deliberate deception that is not dishonest?

Parents telling stories to young children about Father Christmas - The deception is made in good faith without any intention of harming the children.

2. What is an example of an "obvious" fraud, which is not a deception?

A drunken beggar claiming hunger but spending the money he collects on alcohol - It is a fraud to beg for food and spend the money on alcohol, but the pretext is obvious to such an extent that the beggar could not be said to have deceived the giver.

3. What is a "secret profit"?

A payment or commission received by an agent or intermediary in a transaction of which one party to the transaction is not aware.

Chapter 3 – Theft

Theft in context

If this is a book about fraud, why start with theft?

Fraud is a kind of theft, where deception is used. This accounts for the location of statutory fraud in Section16A of the Theft Ordinance.

In seeking to prevent, detect and investigate fraud, what we are looking for may not be fraud at all, but just a form of simple theft.

A straightforward "hand-in-the-till" offence is theft, not fraud, even if it is done behind an employer's back. In this example, trying to not get caught involves deception, but it is a deception used to HIDE the crime (snatching the money). It is not a deception used to DO the crime. It would be the same offence even if the thief snatched the money in front of the eyes of the employer.

All property crimes tend to involve this kind of deception, or "opportunism". There may also be deception used by a dishonest cashier to cover his or her tracks - "Did you do it?" questioned the supervisor, "No," the cashier lied. That denial is deceptive, but not part of the actual offence. It was merely a ploy used to hide the offence and to avoid being detected. Quite often a denial may offer indirect evidence of dishonesty, but it will not offer direct evidence of the offence of stealing.

Fraud features a deception that is actually an essential part of the WAY that the crime is done.

It is important to not become "fraud obsessed". Be aware that you may be dealing with a simple case of theft. Fraud only happens when the deception is part of the actual offence.

HINT:

One of the easiest ways of spotting the difference between these two kinds of deception is to ask, "When did the deception happen?" If the deception happened AFTER the taking of the money, it was probably just done to hide the offence, and this would be a case of theft. If the deception happened BEFORE anything was taken, it may be more essential to the commission of the offence, making it a more likely case of fraud. Fraud is present when there is a causal link between the deception and the unlawful obtaining of property.

Theft Ordinance: s2 "Basic Definition of Theft"

Most non-lawyers are aware that theft, or stealing, means taking something that belongs to someone else. The elements of the crime that offer potential defences and are most important to concentrate on are:

1. That the taking of the property was dishonest; and,
2. That there was an intention of permanently depriving the rightful owner of his possession of the property.

These two factors are sometimes the trickiest to prove in Court. The elements of the offence which need to be proved are set out in s2(1) of the Theft Ordinance:

LAW CHECKLIST

Theft Ordinance – s2(1)

1. "(1) A person commits theft if he
    -   dishonestly
    -   appropriates
    -   property belonging to another
    -   with the intention of permanently depriving the other of it.

Here is the same checklist in diagram form, followed by the statutory definitions.

Chart 8 Theft – S.2, Theft Ordinance

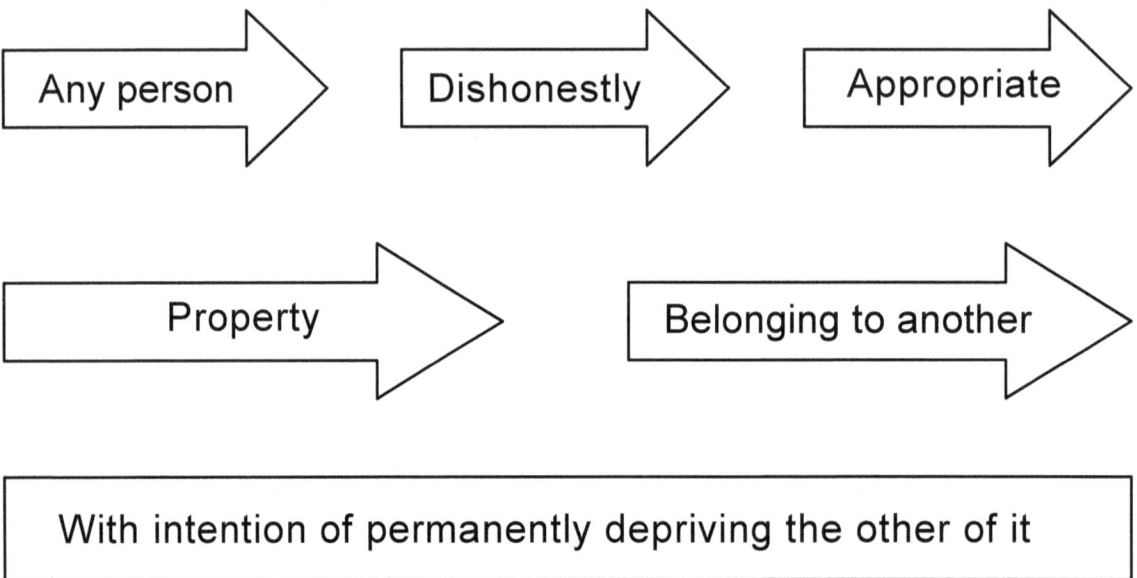

Any person ⟩ Dishonestly ⟩ Appropriate ⟩

Property ⟩ Belonging to another ⟩

With intention of permanently depriving the other of it

With Intention of Permanently Depriving the Other of It

Theft Ordinance: s3 "Dishonestly"

How courts determine "dishonestly" becomes clear by reviewing several prominent cases.

The test of dishonesty in theft offences is well known. It was delineated by the English Court of Appeal in _R v. Ghosh_ [1982] QB 1053. Having reviewed many earlier authorities, Lord Lane LCJ concluded:

> _"In determining whether the prosecution has proved that the defendant was acting dishonestly a jury must first of all decide whether according to the ordinary standards of reasonable and honest people what was done was dishonest. If it was not dishonest by those standards, that is the end of the matter and the prosecution fails. If it was dishonest by those standards, then the jury must consider whether the defendant himself must have realised that what he was doing was by those standards dishonest. In most cases, where the actions are obviously dishonest by ordinary standards, there will be no doubt about it. It will be obvious that the defendant himself knew that he was acting dishonestly. It is dishonest for a defendant to act in a way which he knows ordinary people consider to be dishonest, even if he asserts or genuinely believes that he is morally justified in acting as he did. For example, Robin Hood or those ardent anti-vivisectionists who remove animals from vivisection laboratories are acting dishonestly, even though they may consider themselves to be morally justified in doing what they do, because they know that ordinary people would consider these actions to be dishonest."_

Ghosh provides a two-pronged test. To be considered to have acted "dishonestly", both questions must be answered affirmatively. The questions are:

- Would most people think the action was dishonest?
  (The precise legal phrasing is: "According to the ordinary standards of reasonable and honest people (_was_) what was done...dishonest"?)

  Did the Defendant realise that most people would think it was dishonest?

This is also more formally known as the objective/subjective test, and its two paraphrased component parts question:

1. whether an action was dishonest; and then, also,
2. whether the criminal must have known it was.

Both need to be satisfied affirmatively for the action to be found to have been dishonest as a matter of law.

This decision expands the section 3 explanations, which amount to a set of exclusion examples, that is to say things which are NOT dishonest under the law.

LAW CHECKLIST {Dishonesty Checklist}

<u>Theft Ordinance : s3(1) and s3(2)</u>

1.   "A person's appropriation of property belonging to another is not to be regarded as dishonest-

- (a) if he appropriates the property in the belief that he has in law the right to deprive the other of it, on behalf of himself or of a third person; or
- (b) if he appropriates the property in the belief that he would have the other's consent if the other knew of the appropriation and the circumstances of it; or
- (c) (except where the property came to him as trustee or personal representative) if he appropriates the property in the belief that the person to whom the property belongs cannot be discovered by taking reasonable steps."

This is largely self-explanatory. To paraphrase:

- It is not dishonest to take something if you think you are allowed to, or if you take it for someone else who is allowed to have it;
- It is not dishonest to take something if you think the other person would agree to let you have it;
- Keeping found property is not stealing if reasonable steps would not identify the owner.

This is followed by s3(2)

"(2) A person's appropriation of property belonging to another may be dishonest notwithstanding that he is willing to pay for the property."

This may not apply to the circumstances of some cases. It would apply if, for example, a thief stole a mobile phone but then offered to pay for it when caught, or if the thief originally offered to pay for the mobile phone, but then took it without paying, after changing his mind about the original offer.

Applying the Ghosh test in practice

There are practical problems in the application of the two tests in that so much will depend on the unique experience, preferences, culture, education and other personal characteristics of the jury or, in a 'bench trial' (where the judge is the sole 'trier of fact').

For example, a conservative jury may think that breaking a company's Employee Code of Conduct rules is unforgivable and constitutes evidence of "dishonesty" while a more liberal jury may consider that breaking these rules does not really show dishonesty because it doesn't violate the criminal code.

A judge's instructions to a jury attempt to limit this degree of range in reasoning, but cannot be expected to completely eliminate it. In practice, juries draw upon their own experience and values when determining what's "dishonest".

The practical difficulty in applying the Ghosh test is illustrated by two court cases concerning the unauthorized access to computer systems by government employees to obtain information. Both defendants, an Assistant Assessor of the Inland Revenue Department and a Chief Inspector of Police from the Marine Division, were prosecuted under Crimes Ordinance S. 161. In each instance, the central issue of the case was whether or not the defendant acted dishonestly.

The Inland Revenue Officer had been acquitted at the initial magistracy hearing. On appeal by the prosecution, the High Court directed that the defendant be convicted as the High Court Judge considered what the defendant did was dishonest.

It was accepted that he breached internal rules of the Inland Revenue Department when he obtained the personal data of a female colleague in order to apply for a membership account with a charity, using his own credit card details. Significantly, there was no concealment of his actions.

The Court of Final Appeal held it was up to the Magistrate to decide upon the evidence before him as to whether what the defendant did was honest or dishonest. Hence it reversed the decision of the High Court Judge. The Court of Final Appeal went on to say:

> "Indeed it might well be that he wanted the complainant and possibly other people as well to know that it was he who had done it. This is a conduct which may reasonably be regarded as inconsistent with dishonesty."

In the case of the former Marine Division Chief Inspector of Police, the Court of Final Appeal concluded that there was clear evidence of dishonesty when the defendant instructed a junior officer to obtain access to the personal data of the defendant's former tenant. When confronted by his colleagues the defendant lied that he was collecting the information in connection with an official enquiry.

At the initial hearing Magistrate Wyeth applied the Ghosh test and found:

> "The defendant must have realised ordinary, reasonable and honest people would expect personal information such as Hong Kong Identity Card numbers, addresses and related information collected by or accessible by the Police would not be accessed for other than genuine Police business and that any illegitimate accessing of that information is not honest activity, it is dishonest."[9]

---

9   See, Li Man Wai v. Secretary for Justice – (2003) HKCFA 51.

"I consider by the ordinary standards of reasonable and honest people what was done was dishonest. The circumstances of the gaining of the access, the circumstances of his employment, his age and level of education, which includes tertiary legal education, was such that the defendant must have realised that what he was doing was dishonest by the ordinary standards by reasonable and honest people."[10]

On appeal it was held that "on that evidence the magistrate was entitled to make the finding he did as to dishonesty."

The Court of Final Appeal ultimately decided:

"The charge is based on the sad fact that, while he was a Chief Inspector of Police attached to the Marine Regional Command and Control Centre, he accessed that centre's computer system and obtained there from a certain person's address. He pretended that he was doing so in connection with a Police inquiry in relation to a vessel. In fact, that person was a former tenant of his. Why he wanted his former tenant's address is unknown. It is also plainly irrelevant. He obtained the information for his private purposes by pretending that the information was required in connection with his Police duties. Not only was his conduct unauthorised. The pretence rendered the information gained by such pretence a dishonest gain. That suffices to establish his guilt. What matters is that his purpose was private and not, as he pretended, connected with his Police duties. Beyond that, it does not matter why he wanted the information. So his leave application which is based on the untenable contention that his precise purpose in obtaining the information had to be established and shown to be dishonest independently of how the information was obtained is dismissed.[11]"

These decisions clearly demonstrate the difficulty applying the two-stage test under Ghosh. The impact for fraud investigators is that they should aim to discover the state of mind of the suspect through effective interviews and other means so as to form a firm conclusion as to dishonesty.

Theft Ordinance: s4 "Appropriates"

Under Hong Kong law "appropriation" not only means "taking", but can also refer to a person simply treating something that doesn't belong to him as if it did. A waitress giving customers free desserts (without authorization to do so) offers one example of this type of "appropriation".

This makes it possible for you to be convicted of theft even when you never actually possess the stolen property. Saying, "You can borrow this bike," appropriates the bike if the owner doesn't give you permission to loan it to anybody. This appropriation escalates to theft if you change the terms slightly and say, "You can have this

---

10 HKSAR v. Alistair Charles Currie – [2004] HKCFI 913.

11 Allistair Charles Currie v. HKSAR – [2005] HKCFA 6.

bike". For this hypothesis, as long as the bike recipient does not realise that you are not the true owner, he will be innocent of theft.

LAW CHECKLIST

Theft Ordinance : s4(1) and s4(2)

1. Any assumption by a person of the rights of an owner amounts to an appropriation, and this includes, where he has come by the property (innocently or not) without stealing it, any later assumption of a right to it by keeping or dealing with it as owner.

2. Where property or a right or interest in property is or purports to be transferred for value to a person acting in good faith, no later assumption by him of rights which he believed himself to be acquiring shall, by reason of any defect in the transferor's title, amount to theft of the property.

Theft Ordinance: s5

Section 5 of the Theft Ordinance identifies "property" and, with its quaintly comprehensive coverage, reveals how old the original law is. We will focus on the first sentence but not address the parts that deal with rustic, rural property issues. Persons concerned with leasing land, wild animals and collecting mushrooms are welcome to consult the full text of the statute.

The first sentence broadly defines "all property" to include just about everything. Money, "real" property (as in real estate), personal property and "intangible property" are listed. These wide categories include financial property such as debts and credit notes and intellectual property, like copyright and trade secrets. It is possible then to steal something that cannot be touched, if it has value and can belong to someone. In particular, certain "rights" are viewed as intangible property. Hong Kong export quotas have been held to be property under s5(1)[12]. Despite the broad scope of the definition, confidential information such as the questions and answers to an examination paper, is not regarded as "property" for purposes of charging theft.

As with much of the law it is useful to recognize that the right to call for a service would be considered an intangible property, while the service itself would not be considered property.

LAW CHECKLIST

Theft Ordinance : s5(1)

1. "Property" includes:

    ■   money and

---

12 AG Hong Kong v Nai-Kung [1987] 1 WLR 1339.

- all other property, real and personal, including,
- things in action and other
- intangible property.

Theft Ordinance: s6 "Belonging to Another"

Section 6 covers an assortment of complex issues meriting a technical expatiation that goes beyond the scope of this primer. It is useful to observe that Section Six creates an extended meaning to "belonging to another" to include simply having possession.

This affects "making off without payment" offences, such as filling your car and driving away from a petrol station or leaving a restaurant after finishing a meal without paying. These incidents cannot be addressed as theft because by the time the goods were "appropriated" (as the customer left without paying), the customer already had possession of the goods. Considering the construction of the Theft Ordinance, it is not possible to steal what you already possess. This conundrum gives rise to further legislation with the addition of Theft Ordinance: s18c – Making off without payment.

This legal puzzle permeates fraud and deception offences which often involve theft of items already technically in the possession of the fraudster. In those offences fraud can be charged even though someone is already in possession of the item at the time he commits the fraud. The "making off without payment" cases are often prosecuted under one of the "Obtaining by Deception" sections (see s.18A, B and D), with the rationale that the customer has deceived the proprietor into thinking the petrol or food would be paid for. Section18C, with its specific "Making off without payment" title seems more appropriate for self-service offences where it would strain credulity to argue deception when no human beings were deceived.

Theft Ordinance: s7 "With the intention of permanently depriving the other of it"

Section 7 strives to explain how "intent" is interpreted and applied in the context of theft.

Surprisingly, simple borrowing can be chargeable as theft when the thief is "treating the thing as his own". "Permanently" doesn't necessarily have to mean "forever". "Permanently", in this context is perhaps better conceptually understood as "completely".

The prosecution bears the legal burden to prove each and every legal element of the offence beyond all reasonable doubt. Once there is proof of intent to permanently deprive, we still need to separately prove that the "taking" was dishonest. This is why the word "dishonestly" appears separately in the wording of s3(1).

Proving the offence

To meet their burden of proof, prosecutors must assemble strong and compelling evidence to show the defendant is guilty as charged. Evidence can be direct, like when there is an admission of guilt by the defendant, or circumstantial, as occurs with many complex fraud prosecutions where the court is invited to draw reasonable inferences from thousands of documents.

Presentation of evidence

Fraud investigators need to present their evidence in the most accessible way possible. Effective report writing is essential for the persuasive presentation of evidence.

LAW CHECKLIST

Theft Ordinance - s7(1) and s7(2)

1. A person appropriating property belonging to another without meaning the other permanently to lose the thing itself is nevertheless to be regarded as having the intention of permanently depriving the other of it if his intention is to

   - treat the thing as his own to dispose of regardless of the other's rights; and
   - a borrowing or lending of it may amount to so treating   if,   but   only if, the borrowing or lending of it is for a period and in circumstances making it equivalent to an outright taking or disposal.

2. Without prejudice to the generality of subsection (1),

   - where a person having possession or control (lawfully or not) of property belonging to another,
   - parts with the property under a condition as to its return which he may not be able to perform,
   - this (if done for purposes of his own and without the other's authority)
   - amounts to treating the property as his own to dispose of regardless of the other's rights.

Basically, if you act as if you were the owner, or if you do something with the property that only the owner would normally do, or by your actions make someone else think you are the owner of the property, you will be treated as having shown an intention of permanently depriving the owner of it.

Chapter 4 – Fraud offences

The word "Defraud" in criminal law

The criminal law defines "defraud" as acting: "dishonestly to prejudice or to take the risk of prejudicing another's right, knowing that you have no right to do so."[13]

Statutory Fraud

The relatively new offence of statutory fraud was introduced in Section 16A of the 1970 Theft Ordinance by amendment (16th July, 1999). It is legally quite similar to civil fraud.

The definition of statutory fraud contains a fairly lengthy checklist. Cross-references are explained below:

LAW CHECKLIST

Theft Ordinance - s16A(1)

- "If any person by any deceit (whether or not the deceit is the sole or main inducement)
- and with intent to defraud
- induces another person to commit an act or make an omission, which results either -
  - (a) in benefit to any person other than the second-mentioned person; or
  - (b) in prejudice or a substantial risk of prejudice to any person other than the first-mentioned person,
  - (c) the first-mentioned person commits the offence of fraud and is liable on conviction upon indictment to imprisonment for 14 years."

The fraud section contains a lengthy set of definitions of key words from this checklist, including:

LAW CHECKLIST

Theft Ordinance s16A(2) – "intent to defraud"

"(2) For the purposes of subsection (1), a person shall be treated as having an intent to defraud if,

- at the time when he practises the deceit,
- he intends that he will by the deceit
- (whether or not the deceit is the sole or main inducement)
- induce another person
- to commit an act or make an omission,

---

13 Law Reform Commission of Hong Kong Report on Creation of a Substantive Offence of Fraud.

- which will result in either or both of the consequences referred to in paragraphs (a) and (b) of that subsection.

LAW CHECKLIST

Theft Ordinance s16A(3) –"benefit", "deceit", "prejudice"

"For the purposes of this section -
- «benefit» means any financial or proprietary gain, whether temporary or permanent;
- «deceit» means any deceit (whether deliberate or reckless)
  - by words or conduct
  - (whether by any act or omission)
  - as to fact or as to law,
  - including
    - a deceit relating to the past, the present or the future and
    - a deceit as to the intentions of the person practising the deceit or of any other person;…
- «prejudice» means any financial or proprietary loss, whether temporary or permanent."

This then is the key fraud offence, where deception is used to commit a theft or to gain some kind of economic advantage or cause loss to another. In this framework, if property has been taken, the person committing the fraud must have put himself or anyone else except the victim in a better position financially or in relation to valuable property. This offence is likely to be the first one the investigator will consider.

Points to Note

The use of the word "or" at the end of s16(1)(a) means that we only need to prove one of these results ("prejudice" or "benefit"), not both.

Financial loss or property damage are the qualifying consequences to complete the offence of statutory fraud. Other kinds of "advantage" or "disadvantage» to legal rights do not qualify.

Intent to use deception to cause that person a financial loss, or someone else a financial benefit must also be proven. Dishonesty is not listed as one of the required proof components, but considering the general definition of "defraud" at the beginning of this chapter, one realises evidence of dishonesty will always be worth presenting as part of the investigation.

Chart 9 - Fraud – S.16A, Theft Ordinance

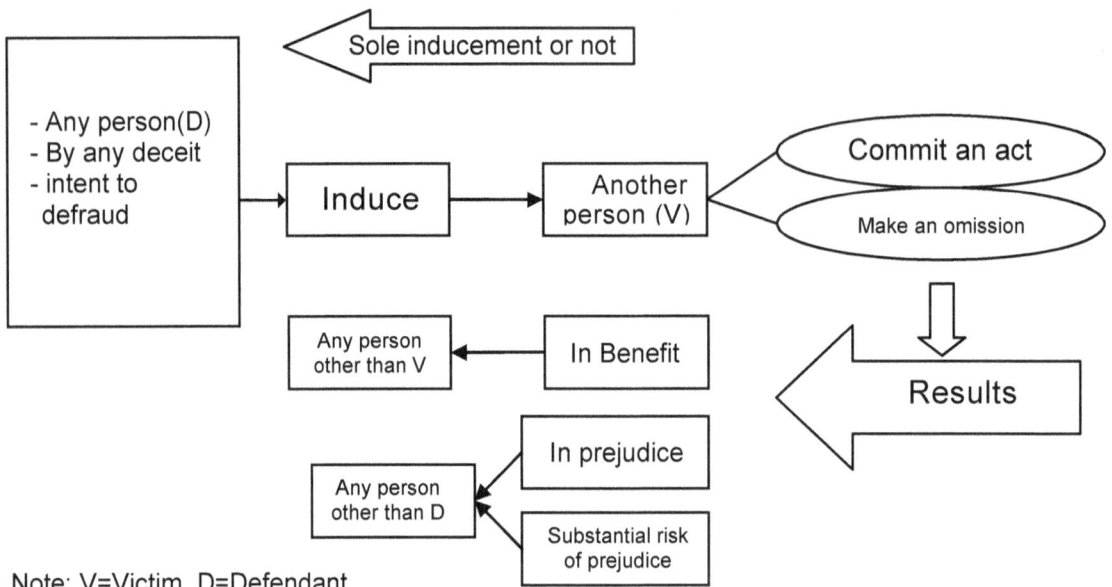

- Any person(D)
- By any deceit
- intent to defraud

Sole inducement or not

Induce → Another person (V)

Commit an act

Make an omission

Any person other than V ← In Benefit

In prejudice

Any person other than D

Substantial risk of prejudice

Results

Note: V=Victim, D=Defendant

Obtaining by Deception - Theft Ordinance: s17, s18, s18A, s18B

The second set of statutory offences involving fraud is the "Obtaining by Deception" offences. At first sight it might seem there is little to distinguish these from fraud as discussed above. The focus of this category is on "obtaining" in particular. These offences arise in situations where the deception tricks the owner into giving away his property voluntarily.

Despite these differences, it is best to understand that there are considerable over-laps between each of the fraud and obtaining offences, and between all these offences and theft. This duplication is non-problematic, as law professionals will decide which offence to charge based on the facts of each particular case.

Section 17 - Obtaining Property by Deception

This offence focuses on simple deceptions used to obtain property such as borrow-ing a library book and giving a false address or identity, then never returning it. In other words, where deception is used as part of a straightforward theft, tricking the owner into giving up possession voluntarily. Dishonesty is included in s17(1) as an element of the offence. The offence set out in Section 17 of the Theft Ordinance is defined as follows:

LAW CHECKLIST

Theft Ordinance - s17(1)

- "Any person who
    - by any deception (whether or not such deception was the sole or main inducement)
    - dishonestly
    - obtains property
    - belonging to another,
    - with the intention of permanently depriving the other of it,
    - shall be guilty of an offence and shall be liable on conviction upon indictment to imprisonment for 10 years."

Chart 10 - Obtaining Property by Deception – S.17(1), Theft Ordinance

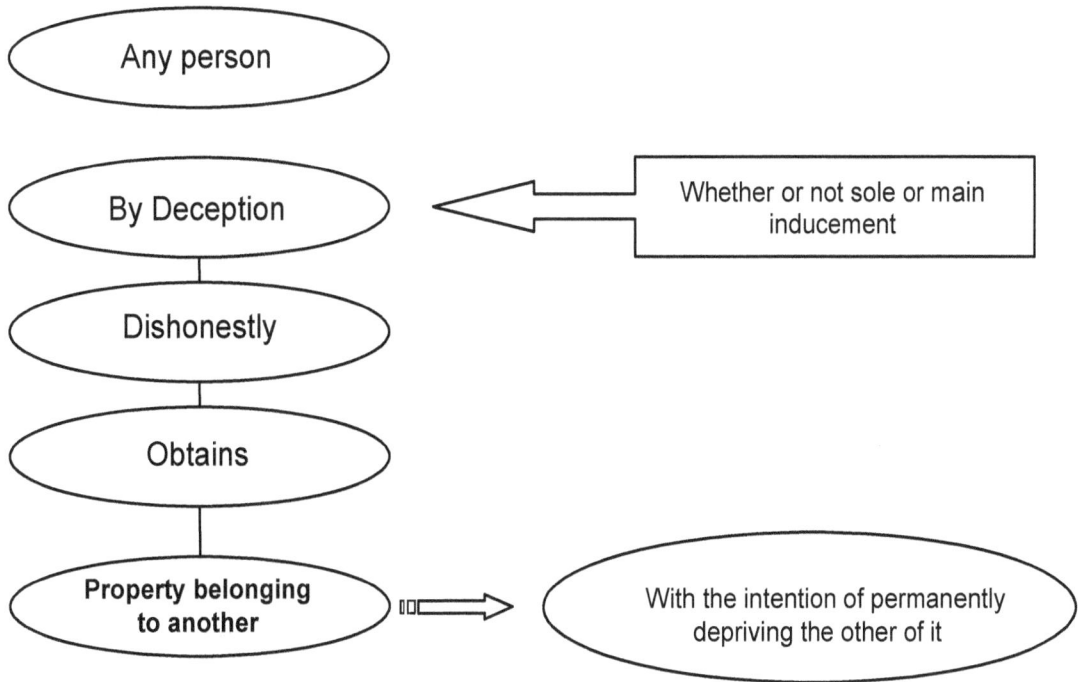

Any person

By Deception

Whether or not sole or main inducement

Dishonestly

Obtains

Property belonging to another

With the intention of permanently depriving the other of it

The rest of the section defines some of the terms used above, with s17(4) perhaps being the most important.

Chart 11 - Definition of Deception – S.17 (4), Theft Ordinance

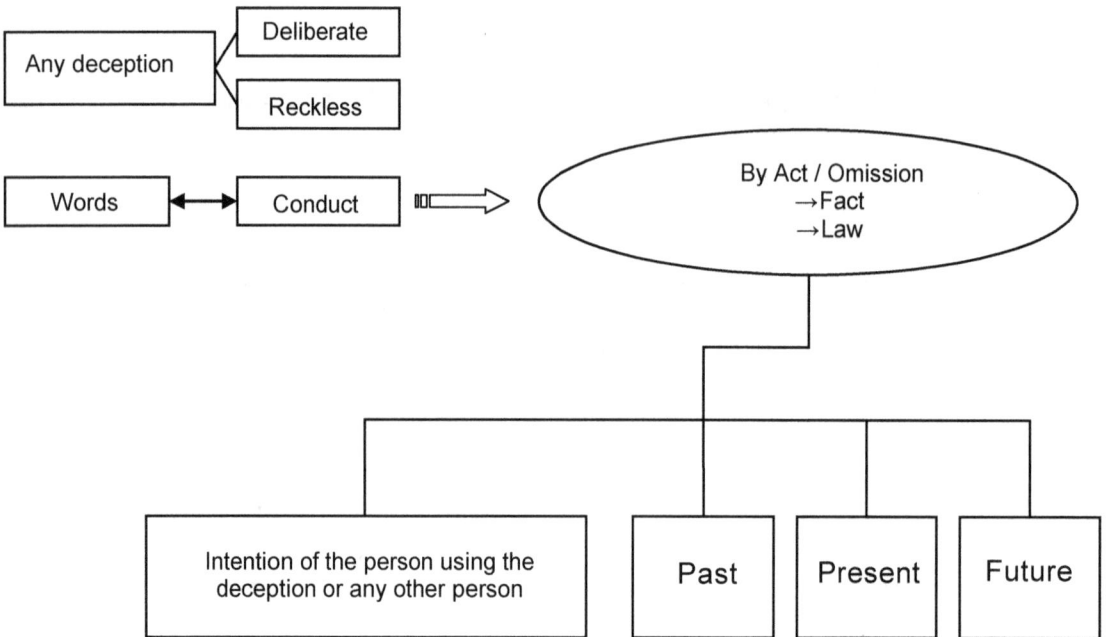

LAW CHECKLIST

Theft Ordinance - s17(4)

"For the purposes of this section-
- «deception» means any deception (whether deliberate or reckless)
- by words or conduct (whether by any act or omission)
- as to fact or as to law,
- including
  - a deception relating to the past, the present or the future and
  - a deception as to the intentions of the person using the deception or any other person."

Section 18 - Obtaining pecuniary advantage by deception

This offence concerns cases where someone obtains a loan, overdraft or some other kind of financial facility on false pretences. A specific list of the situations to which this offence applies is set out in the section.

LAW CHECKLIST

Theft Ordinance - s18(1)

"Any person who
- by any deception (whether or not such deception was the sole or main inducement)

- dishonestly obtains
- for himself or another
- any pecuniary advantage
- shall be guilty of an offence and shall be liable on conviction upon indictment to imprisonment for 10 years."

The list of the situations to which this offence applies is then set out in s18(2).

Chart 12 - Obtaining pecuniary advantage by deception S. 18, Theft Ordinance

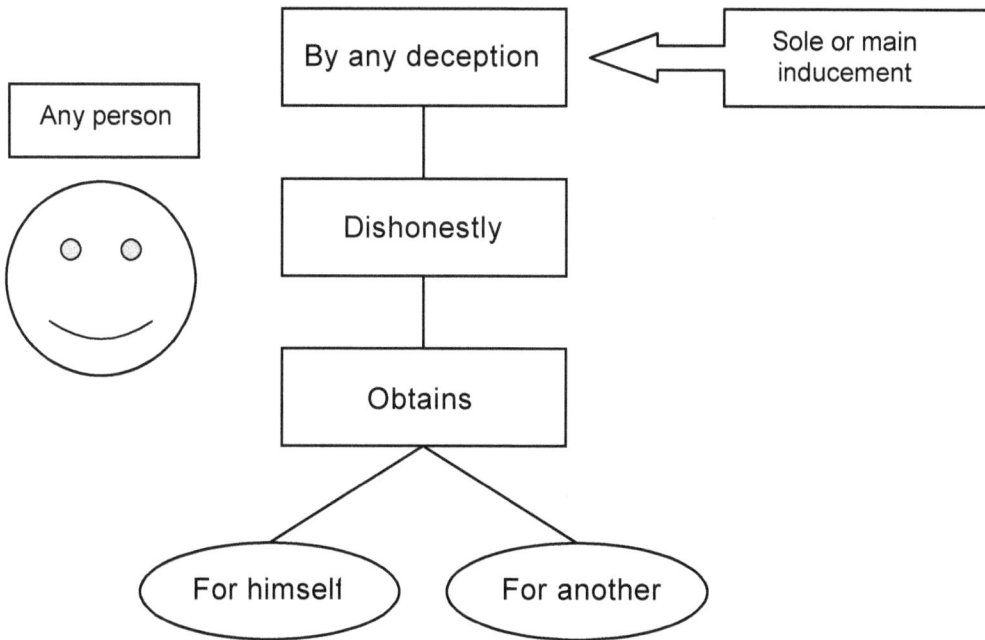

LAW CHECKLIST

Theft Ordinance - s18(2)

The cases in which a pecuniary advantage within the meaning of this section is to be regarded as obtained for a person are cases where –
- a) he is granted by a bank or deposit-taking company, or
- b) any subsidiary thereof the principal business of which is the provision of credit –
  - I. a credit facility or credit arrangement;
  - II. an improvement to, or extension of, the terms of a credit facility or credit arrangement; or
  - III. a credit to, or a set off against, an account,
  - IV. whether any such credit facility, credit arrangement or account –
  - V. is in his name or the name of another person; or
  - VI. is legally enforceable or not; (Added 46 of 1986 s. 2)he is allowed to borrow
- c) by way of overdraft, or
- d) to take out any policy of insurance or annuity contract, or
- e) obtain an improvement on the terms which he is allowed to do so,

f) whether any such overdraft, policy of insurance or annuity contract –
　　I. is in his name or the name of another person; or
　　I. is legally enforceable or not; or (Replaced 46 of 1986 s.2)

He is given the opportunity to earn remuneration or greater remuneration in an office or employment, or to win money by betting.

Chart 13 - Definition of pecuniary advantage S.18 (2) (a)-(c)

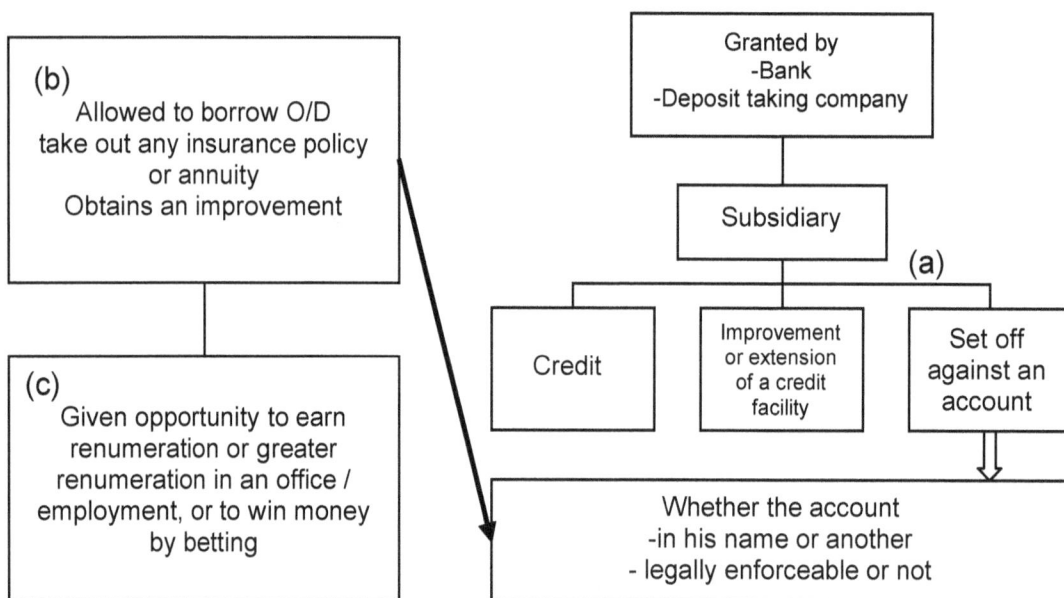

Section 18A - Obtaining services by deception

The target of this section is to examine whether services, usually valued professional services, are obtained by deception for the fraudster or for someone else. This covers cases in which what is exploited or taken is valuable, but is not property, such as a dry cleaning service or a plane journey.

LAW CHECKLIST

Theft Ordinance - s18A(1)

1. A person who

   ▪ by any deception (whether or not such deception was the sole or main inducement)
   ▪ dishonestly
   ▪ obtains services
   ▪ from another
   ▪ shall be guilty of an offence and shall be liable on conviction upon indictment to imprisonment for 10 years.

LAW CHECKLIST

Theft Ordinance - s18A(2)

2. It is an obtaining of services where

- the other is induced to confer a benefit by
- doing some act,
- or causing or permitting some act to be done,
- on the understanding that the benefit has been or will be paid for.

Section 18B - Evasion of liability by deception

This offence focuses not on the original obtaining of a benefit or something of value, but on the subsequent evasion of liability for it by deception.

LAW CHECKLIST

Theft Ordinance - s18B(1)

"Subject to subsection (2), where a person by any deception (whether or not such deception was the sole or main inducement) -

a. dishonestly secures the remission of the whole or part of any existing liability to make a payment, whether his own liability or another's;

b. with intent to make default (whether the default is permanent or otherwise) in whole or in part on any existing liability to make a payment, or with intent to let another do so, dishonestly induces the creditor or any person claiming payment on behalf of the creditor to wait for payment (whether or not the due date for payment is deferred) or to forgo payment; or

c. dishonestly obtains any exemption from or abatement of liability to make a payment,

d. he shall be guilty of an offence and shall be liable on conviction upon indictment to imprisonment for 10 years."

The reference to s18B(2) is a reference to the requirement that the "liability" in question be one that is legally enforceable.

Conspiracy to defraud at common law

Chart 14 - Conspiracy to Defraud

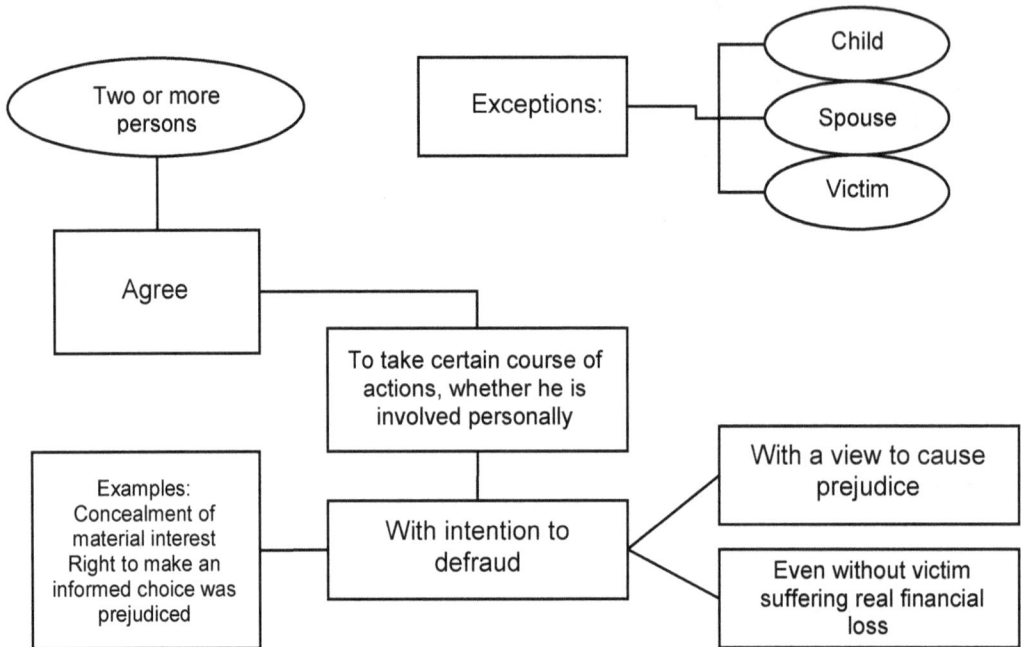

The offence of conspiracy to defraud at common law was specifically preserved at the time that statutory fraud under s16A was introduced by way of a 1999 amendment to the Theft Ordinance. This old, common law offence has been the frequent subject of criticism, but it remains an important part of Hong Kong law because of its flexibility.

The scope of the offence is broad and it lacks a clear definition. This, combined with its conspiracy component, has attracted most of the criticisms. Conspiracy, as discussed earlier, means that the offence cannot be committed by a single individual.

Conspiracy to defraud was historically described as involving "any deceitful practice in defrauding, or endeavouring to defraud, a man of his known right by some artful device, contrary to the plain rules of common honesty." However, that eighteenth century reference to deception is no longer part of the modern criminal law, which focuses simply on the dishonesty of the scheme.

An accepted definition in modern times was presented by Viscount Dilhorne *in Scott v Metropolitan Police Commissioner* [1975] AC 819, at 1039, where he defined a conspiracy to defraud as simply being, "An agreement by two or more by dishonesty to deprive a person of something which is his or to which he is or would or might be entitled, or....an agreement by two or more dishonestly to injure some proprietary right."

The conspiracy element is completed by the agreement to do the act, whether or not the fraud actually gets off the ground, and whether or not any deception is involved.

There can be a fine line between a criminal act and an acceptable level of "commercial sharp practice" that is considered by many to be an important part of an energetic and competitive business community. The uncertainty does not make for good law and is not good for business. The adaptability can frequently benefit law enforcement.

It is all too common for an uneducated corporate executive of a listed corporation in Hong Kong, who may well be a successful businessman from Mainland China, to be ensnared by this offence, often after following bad advice from individuals who, after being approached by the authorities, quickly turn to become witnesses for the prosecution in exchange for immunity from prosecution.

There is a pressing need to educate corporate executives lacking knowledge of the Hong Kong criminal law related to fraud. Their retained learned and educated advisers, better known as licensed "Sponsors" or "Corporate Financiers", should also be brought current on the laws relating to fraud, especially Conspiracy to Defraud.

Chapter 5 – Prevention

Introduction: Fraud and Fraud Prevention in Hong Kong

Fraud continues to be a growing problem in the world[14]. Whether this is also the case in Hong Kong is difficult to determine. Interestingly, when police statistics are analysed, fraud is one of the only offences which has been rising there over the last few decades. The Hong Kong Police Force distinguishes between three types of fraud, they are: 1) deception; 2) business fraud; and, 3) forgery and coinage. These three categories do not offer a perfect reflection of all the reported fraud related cases in Hong Kong. Embezzlement, for example, might be a form of fraud which is not recorded in police statistics as fraud. Statistics on the number of reported fraud cases do offer an indication of general fraud trends. Between 1988 and 2008, the number of reported fraud cases rose from 1585 to 5863[15]. Hong Kong Police Force crime statistics show an increase in deception crimes from 2008 to 2010, with a slight decrease from 2010 to 2011.

Available surveys attempting to measure Hong Kong fraud are not comprehensive and are not particularly scientific. Government surveys will want to document a healthy, fraud-free business environment; commercial surveys by security consulting firms or financial services providers may have their own biases. In their **11th Global Fraud Survey** (published in 2010) Ernst & Young's Fraud Investigation & Dispute Services sought out chief financial officers (CFOs) and heads of internal audit, legal and compliance to get their views on how companies are managing risks associated with fraud, bribery and corruption. More than 1,400 interviews were conducted in 36 countries (including China and Hong Kong). Their survey

---

14 The report prepared for the UK Home Office and Serious Fraud Office in 2000 by NERA, "The Economic Cost of Fraud" (March 2000) put the cost to the UK, including resource costs in its calculation, at over six billion pounds sterling, that is, over HK$84 billion. In their 2007 report, the (UK) Association of Chief Police Officers (ACPO) identified direct fraud losses of £13 billion during 2005. Using fraud figures that are currently available, in their Annual Fraud Indicator report from January 2010, the (UK) National Fraud Authority (NFA) estimates that fraud cost the UK economy £30.5 billion during 2008. PricewaterhouseCoopers' Global Economic Crime Survey in 2005 yielded key findings where: 45% of companies reported falling victim to fraud in the past two years; on average they recorded suffering an average of 8 serious incidents; Since 2003 there has been: a 71% increase in the number of companies reporting cases of corruption & bribery; a 133% increase in the number reporting money laundering; and a 140% increase in the number reporting financial misrepresentation; Fraud involving a loss of assets cost companies—on average—over US$ 1.7 million, which was a 50% increase over 2003; 40% suffered significant loss of reputation, decreased staff motivation, and damaged business relations. Ernst & Young Fraud Investigation & Dispute Services 11th Global Fraud Survey (2010) lists an average increase to 16% respondents reporting recent (within the past two years) experience of fraud, up from 13% in 2008.

15 Royal Hong Kong Police (1989), Crime and Enforcement Report 1988; Hong Kong Police Force (2009), Crime in Hong Kong 2008.

identified a global, average increase of company fraud experience within the preceding two years of 16%, up from 13% in 2008. Significantly, none of the business division functions interviewed had full confidence in all aspects of their fraud and corruption risk management strategies. Their findings are specifically related to the private sector, but are also relevant to the public sector and non-governmental organizations, both of which encounter many of the same fraud and corruption issues.

Dissimilar definitions of fraud contribute to the challenge of quantifying and comparing fraud incidence internationally. Also, reasonably apprehensive about commercial blowback, many companies are simply unwilling to report fraud, skewing realistic fraud incidence figures. Some commercial surveys seem to indicate South East Asia may be a region in denial about fraud.

This is reinforced in the Ernst & Young 11th Global Fraud Survey, which observes the frequency of fraud risk assessments was lowest in the Far East with a 25% of respondents in that region stating they never conducted a preventative assessment. Nearby Japan was the only sub-region scoring lower, with a 30% "never assess" rate.

According to PricewaterhouseCoopers (PwC) 2009 Global Economic Crime Survey, the number of fraud cases in Hong Kong was very low compared to other economies[16]. The report shows that only 13% of the 100 companies surveyed in Hong Kong had experienced fraud in the preceding 12 months, while the global average was 30%. PwC concludes that the rise could be explained by a rise in fraud cases, but also correctly observes that greater awareness might also have contributed to higher discovery and reporting levels.

In the absence of awareness, fraud often remains undetected and unreported. A 2000 survey in the UK found that only 5.8% of the discovered cases of fraud were reported[17]. In a 2005 PwC survey, only 44% of fraud incidents were ever referred to law enforcement agencies, and only 14% of those fraudsters were ultimately convicted, as contrasted to a global conviction rate of 29%.

When there is a violent crime, there is a corpse, an injury, or a missing person. Property crimes like theft involve observable loss. The crime by deception that is fraud frequently goes entirely undetected, further compounding efforts to measure its true impact.

PwC surveys have found high reported levels of _corruption_ in Hong Kong, attributing this high incidence not to greater levels of corruption, but to the successful

---

16 PwC (2009), The Global Economic Crime Survey: Economic crime in a downturn, November 2009, London: PricewaterhouseCoopers.

17 NERA (March 2000), "The Economic Cost of Fraud", chapter 6, p57, calculation derived from Table 6.1.2.

investigation and enforcement work of the Independent Commission Against Corruption (ICAC) in Hong Kong.

The preferred approach to fraud seeks to prevent it from happening in the first place. "There is simply no substitute for a person's awareness and wariness"[18]. This is not just a matter of business prudence, it is also, in certain cases, a regulatory requirement, as all listed corporations are expected to conduct an annual review of their internal control systems to ensure that they are efficient. This necessarily includes a close examination of a corporation's fraud risk management programme.

However, deciding precisely which forms of fraud control, and at what level to implement them on involves the balancing of several cost-benefit considerations, along with a determination of the "fraud (or "fraud risk") tolerance level" of the organization. The UK National Audit Office has stated that, "A major obstacle to developing a fraud response is the absence of a clear assessment of what might constitute an acceptable level of the risk of fraud. From a purely financial point of view, a decision about the level of acceptable risk would be determined based on the scale of potential loss and the cost of preventative and detective controls."[19]

In a UK Attorney General's 2006 Fraud Review, the authors acknowledge both points of view, stating that, "It is our view that the public sector should take a zero tolerance approach to fraud," and going on to say, "...that is, where the known losses to, and risks of, fraud outweigh the cost of preventing and detecting that fraud, then action should be taken." While apparently contradictory, these remarks do usefully present both ends of the range of approaches to developing a fraud control strategy, and to determining a fraud "tolerance level" in particular. Clearly, the issue requires careful thought and clear decisions.

It is necessary then to combine these decisions into an integrated strategic approach. There are three broad elements to prevention:

- systems and controls;
- deterrence; and
- compliance culture.

Systems and Controls

Fraud committed by staff and others within an organisation can and should be prevented by good internal and external systems and controls. Fraud committed by those outside the organisation is harder to detect. It is important for a balance to be struck between fraud control and the day-to-day carrying on of business. While extremely efficient systems can be developed and will, in part, be run by external

---

18 Arthur Levitt, US Securities & Exchange Commission, cited in the UK Government's 2005 Fraud Review.

19 UK National Audit Office (2006), "Department for Culture, Media and Sport: Tackling External Fraud in Grant Making", cited at para 6.18, p122, of UK Attorney General's "Fraud Review" (2006).

professionals such as accountants and auditors, their proper operation has the potential to divert a disproportionate amount of labour, time and resources away from internal business functions. This sometimes fails a cost-benefit analysis.

There may also be morale issues of human disincentive within the organisation– it was United States President Harry Truman who said, "When you have efficient government, you have a dictatorship."

It is for these reasons we highlight other matters in addition to systems and controls in this chapter. Internal and external controls remain the starting point of fraud prevention, but it is important to be alert to the possibility of indirect costs that are greater than those attributable to the original fraud problem itself. It is also important to maintain a broad and comprehensive strategy that goes beyond the issue of control.

Deterrence

Effective fraud deterrence is achieved by demonstrating serious consequences for the perpetrators of fraud, together with an energetic approach towards asset recovery. These policies promote an environment that inhibits fraud. Although there are also cost consequences here, they are justified.

Compliance Culture

It has been said that: "Fraud prevention involves more than compiling anti-fraud policies. It also involves the maintenance of an ethical environment that encourages staff at all levels to actively participate…"[20] "Compliance culture" is a key component of modern fraud prevention. It is the positive side of deterrence. It includes training for employees in systems and regulatory compliance, ethics, and the encouragement of whistle-blowing. Such training is best combined with positive role-modelling, reinforcing events and other measures designed to positively enhance the creation of an environment where fraud will be less likely to occur.

It is essential that all of these approaches be integrated into a single, comprehensive fraud strategy.

---

20 Brian Glicksman, UK Treasury Officer of Accounts, quoted in "Good Practice in Tackling External Fraud" (2004) UK National Audit Office, p33.

Integrated Fraud Strategy

An integrated and strategic approach to tackling fraud is consistent with the requirements of good corporate governance, and can itself be part of the corporate communications package for staff and others.

The first step in the development of an Integrated Fraud Strategy is to address the following questions:

Does the organisation -
- Take a strategic approach to tackling fraud risk?
- Assess the size of the threat from internal and external fraud separately and, where significant, undertake a specific risk assessment of each particular threat?
- Identify areas most vulnerable to the risk of fraud?
- Know the size of the fraud threat, the type of fraud committed, who or what class of person is committing the fraud and how often and how much is involved?
- Have a package of measures in place to prevent, detect and recover fraud losses?
- Allocate an annual budget or spending target to its fraud strategy?
- Have targets to stabilize or reduce fraud?
- Allocate responsibilities within the organisation to individuals tasked with tackling fraud risks to ensure that risks are managed, plans are implemented and progress is monitored?

An integrated fraud strategy can be outlined after addressing and answering these questions. The main elements of the strategy can be identified with the acronym "AIR", which stands for ASSESS, IMPLEMENT and REVIEW. The elements are -

1. ASSESS - RISK ASSESSMENT:
- Identify areas of vulnerability;
- Undertake specific fraud risk assessments;
- Estimate the scale of the threat; and
- Understand the type of fraud risk.

2. IMPLEMENT - ANTI-FRAUD MEASURES:
- Assign responsibilities for tracking fraud;
- Allocate resources to a package of effective anti-fraud measures including the three elements identified above and further discussed below;
- Set targets;
- Communicate internally and externally to deter fraud;
- Detect and investigate frauds that do occur; and
- Impose sanctions and consequences.

3. REVIEW – REPORTS AND CONCLUSIONS:
- Monitor performance and targets;

- Review risk assessments over time or as circumstances change;
- Evaluate effectiveness of sanctions;
- Report on progress and conclusions at regular intervals, usually annually; and
- Review the Integrated Fraud Strategy in the light of each annual review.

A key part of the process is the proactive identification of areas of risk and vulnerability. An integrated fraud strategy will then need to consider the three main areas of approach to prevention, to decide on the best combination for the organisation and the particular risks that have been identified.

Compliance Culture

The objective of a compliance culture is to create an environment in which fraud is less likely to occur. A compliance culture is cost-effective, and once established, requires less direct company supervision than other methods of fraud prevention. The focus and emphasis of a compliance culture is on the employee. Compliance is a personal and personnel issue.

It is for this reason that establishing a positive compliance environment also presents an opportunity for the company to reinforce the self-value and personal recognition of each employee. There are, therefore, broader benefits.

It must be emphasized that setting up a compliance culture training and events programme is not enough. The traditional carrot-and-stick approach also requires that an effective deterrent be demonstrated hand in hand with the compliance culture.

Compliance cultures will typically promote and reward 5 features:
- Personal integrity;
- Professional ethics;
- System compliance;
- Regulatory compliance; and
- Whistle-blowing.

The "compliance path" therefore moves out from the centre. It begins with the individual's integrity and self-auditing, and expands through system-based auditing into an integration with company systems and controls to participation in any "whistle-blowing" that may arise.

Personal integrity: In a compliance culture, positive role-modelling must present integrity not merely as a praiseworthy human attribute, but also as the valuable business asset that it is.

Business operations and professional relationships, including those with customers, are largely based on trust. Trust is a valuable business asset. To be able to demonstrate trust in a business requires particular attention to detail. That is to say, trust evolves from the simple ability to do what you say you will do, when you say you will do it, and to be whom you purport to be. Trust comes not from the ability to not make mistakes, but rather from being honest about mistakes that are made.

In corporate or organizational terms, it is essential that the promotion of trust be a two-way process:

- The company must behave in a trustful and respectful way to its employees, and deliver on promises that it makes; and
- Particular attention must be paid to the concept of "leadership", with management and executives understanding, demonstrating *and communicating* their commitment to the principle of trust, as a priority.

With these values in mind, the promotion of attributes such as "trust" and "personal integrity" within an organisation should include:

Positive role-modelling and rewards

- *Communication:* Promotion of positive role-model profiles throughout the organization.

-
- *Events:* This does not mean "trust" workshops, which may be seen as patronizing. A training session on "Body Language", however, is useful and carries the important indirect message that dishonesty is difficult to conceal.

-
- *Messages and Mission Statements:* Active and repeated communication of relevant messages to staff through internal bulletins, general mission statements and at staff meetings.

Professional ethics:

While trust must be cultivated rather than taught, it is wrong to say that professional ethics cannot be taught. Professional ethics are the "trust code" applied and agreed to in formal terms by a profession or industry. They comprise a set of written or spoken rules that business professionals are required to follow. Compliance requires:

- knowledge of the rules;
- self-auditing; and
- additional skills or methods for particular job roles.

These things *can* be taught and coached. Adherence levels indicate increased professionalism and is a business asset. They also convey "business confidence".

Ethical issues become more complicated at the borderlines of aggressive conduct and sharp practice. Ethics training teaches employees how to react to the difficult problems that may arise in such grey areas. People are taught how to identify and react to "conflicts". A lack of proper ethics training can leave employees being overly-cautious when operating in such areas, and can inhibit their performance and appropriate commercial aggression. By removing these impediments to performance through ethics training, employee confidence can be cultivated.

Staff should be provided with a core document, whether it is a set of guidelines or a code of ethics. Training and case-based practice study is also important. It is one small step from sharp practice to fraud and a solid ethics education programme should be part of any effective compliance culture.

System compliance: Useful lateral support for internal and external control systems can be provided by a compliance culture. The effective functioning of the organization's fraud-control systems will demonstrate "compliance in action". These daily or routine procedures require time and employee input, creating a necessary diversion from their main job duties. In the modern business environment other stakeholders, such as insurers, clients and business partners, have to be communicated.

A compliance culture involves higher levels of "transparency" in the way systems are set up and run. Transparency conforms with current standards of good corporate governance, and is an important feature of the modern requirement for "openness".

Regulatory compliance: Regulatory compliance provides practical teeth to the compliance regime and can be considered as an extension of system compliance that requires a proactive approach. Regulations and official guidance notes change, and ignorance of the updated law offers no defence. It is vitally important to keep current information through contacts with relevant regulatory bodies and the associated trade press.

Whistle-blowing: In the US it has been estimated that 30% of frauds are discovered with information from whistle-blowers[21]. Whistle-blowing is a vitally important part of both the prevention and detection of fraud world-wide. It is appropriate for companies to develop and publish a written policy and procedure for whistle-blowing.[22]

Challenges must be acknowledged. These important problems include a natural reluctance to "get involved" or to turn people in. There is also the risk of very real damage to organizational morale with a "watch your back" environment. Other significant issues may arise, connected with the seniority of the fraudster, or worry that the whistle-blower's message will be intercepted or disseminated, compromising the whistle-blower's own interests.

---

21 "Policies and Procedures to Prevent Fraud and Embezzlement: Guidance, Internal Controls, and Investigation" Edward McMillian (Wiley, US: 2006), p.3.

22 Report to the Nations on Occupational Fraud and Abuse, the 2010 Global Fraud Study by the Association of Certified Fraud Examiners.

Alternatively, those who do not reveal important information become arguably complicit in the fraudulent acts. Whistle-blowing can be presented as the best natural consequence of coming into possession of incriminating information.

Devices exist to deal with some of the problems raised above. An anonymous hotline offers a secure delivery for a potentially important source of information. Another method is to provide such a secure tips website, either on intranet or internet. Whistle-blowing should also be rewarded, and the subject of positive role-modelling.

It is important to reinforce the message that prevention is not something that exists in isolation from the detection or the investigation of fraud. A simple checklist can be comprised for the whistle-blower:

If you are not a compliance or legal officer –

- Immediately report the problem to a legal or compliance officer. Your first step should be the company, not law enforcement agencies or regulators, unless the suspected fraud is very high-level;
- Do not destroy documents (either electronic or hardcopy);
- Speed is essential. Without the element of surprise, recovery of incriminating evidence and assets becomes more difficult; and
- Do not attempt to deal with or confront the fraudster.

If you are a lawyer or legal/compliance officer –

- Immediately take steps to preserve and copy documents;
- Seek external assistance from computer forensic experts in the preservation of computer evidence;
- Attempt to suspend the consequences of any ongoing illegal conduct;
- Consider what steps may be taken to recover assets before the fraudster becomes aware of the discovery of the fraud;
- If senior management is involved in the fraud, contact the Board of Directors directly;
- If Directors are involved in the fraud, consider carefully to whom disclosure may properly be made and, as a last resort, consider going directly to the Police or the Independent Commission Against Corruption (ICAC)[23]; and
- Obtain approval to initiate a prompt internal investigation.

In addition, as has been said, it is useful to set up an anonymous hotline and/or website for whistle-blowers. The hotline should be recorded and transcribed, but guaranteed free of number-tracing. Likewise, the website should not log the IP addresses of visitors, and should be an "https" address[24].

---

23 The scenario is not unknown. In November 2004 10 top executives of the Hong Kong company Skyworth Digital Holdings, including their chairman and financial controller, were arrested by the ICAC for corruption and fraud.

24 See for example the UK's «Report a Cheat On-line Form» at https://secure.dwp.gov.uk/benefitfraud/.

Non-anonymous whistle-blowers should also be assisted with their cooperation with any ongoing investigation, and no distinction should be made between overt and anonymous whistle-blowers in the reward programme.

Whistle-blowing is an important part of compliance culture. As an important component of compliance in action, it should be encouraged and the subject of positive role-modelling. It is also an important part of the implementation of the following section, deterrence.

Deterrence

Deterrence works by alerting would-be fraudsters of: (i) an increased likelihood of being discovered; and (ii) the demonstration of serious consequences for those who are discovered.

An effective compliance culture that includes the encouragement of whistle-blowing, together with the implementation of effective internal controls will make the perpetration of fraud more difficult and more likely to be discovered. These are deterrents in themselves.

However, the more commonly recognized form of deterrence is the demonstration of serious consequences for transgressors. These fall into three categories:

- Disciplinary;
- Criminal or Civil; and
- Asset recovery.

Disciplinary consequences

Given the serious nature of fraud, it might be thought uncommon for the consequences to be limited to internal disciplinary measures. In reality disciplinary measures are often the main form of redress. In employment law, fraud will always satisfy the test for gross misconduct and be sufficient to justify instant dismissal. Company contracts may also provide for a loss of retrospective as well as future benefits, depending on the terms of the contract. There may however be cases where less drastic disciplinary action may be taken. Whatever course is chosen, it is essential that internal disciplinary consequences ensue in all cases of fraud. If prompt disciplinary action is not taken, there is no effective deterrence.

Criminal or civil proceedings

Either or both sets of proceedings may result from a case of fraud. It is important that proactive investigation of the incident and collection of evidence occur at the moment of discovery. It will usually be appropriate to contact outside investigators to ensure a proper level of professionalism for these enquiries. Unprofessionally collected evidence may be excluded by both civil and criminal courts. Effective prosecutions require not only a commitment to pursue and win them, but a strong commitment to proper collection and preservation of evidence and co-operation with any external investigation.

<u>Asset Recovery</u>

The cost of asset recovery may sometimes exceed the value of the assets recovered. It is important to bear in mind, however, that asset recovery is also a part of deterrence, and therefore should not simply be analysed on a cost-benefit basis. Long-term policy benefits are also important to consider with deterrence in mind. In most jurisdictions, for example, fraudulent gains are unprotected by bankruptcy or insolvency proceedings and, as long as the civil limitation bar has not fallen, assets may be pursued with all the mechanisms provided by law, including the use of Mareva injunctions and tracing remedies.

It should also be noted that both criminal and civil courts may make compensation orders.

Systems and Controls

There are two broad categories of control systems for fraud prevention – internal and external. The primary object of internal and external controls is to remove the opportunity for fraud. Both should be augmented by risk assessment programmes.

Risk assessment is an essential preliminary step in developing effective controls because these controls will focus on the risk areas, as well as provide regulation across the whole system.

Overall business "risk" is defined as:

> *"The chance of something happening that will have a negative impact on objectives."* *Risk is measured in terms of consequence and likelihood [AS/NZS 4360 (1999) - The 1st business risk management system standard world-wide].*

Before assessing general business risk, it is necessary to identify the organization's objectives. If there is no potential impact on these objectives, no business risk is assessed. Other more specialized categories of risk exist, such as "enterprise business risk", in which the "impact on ability to deliver on strategies" offers another risk assessment criterion.

Obviously, "fraud risk" is another such sub-category. However, it should be noted that in a fraud risk assessment, the risk that is being assessed is limited to the risk of the incidence of fraud. It is not necessary as part of such a risk assessment to assess impact on objectives. It is simply necessary to assess the likelihood of such an event to occur, along with its possible consequences.

It has been said of risk assessment that the approach should be: "Working out-wards from objectives... trying to imagine every possible threat, every imaginable mishap, misunderstanding, external threat, internal error, malpractice, even think-ing the unthinkable."[25] This involves the use of checklists, vulnerability assessments and scenario planning.

In addition to identifying areas of vulnerability within the organization, supply chain and money flow, risk assessment may also include staff profiling and a listing of "employees at risk". Employees under emotional or financial stress, or who have obsessive/compulsive behaviour patterns (including work addiction), or who have "under-achieved" are some of the recognized risk profiles. The overall profile of the Hong Kong fraudster is male (87%), between 31 and 51 (75%), with an education at least to degree level (67%)[26].

Internal and external controls should be developed in consultation with accountants and auditors, as well as professional fraud examiners. Several publications also outline control models, and advice is available from government agencies such as the ICAC, PCO[27] and professional bodies such as the Association of Certified Fraud Examiners and Institute of Internal Auditors[28].

Internal Controls

Internal control refers to formal systems that are designed and implemented to track and check the flow of money, goods and services into, out of, and within an organization. More than 50% of recent reported frauds in Hong Kong recorded in the PwC survey were committed by company employees. This is also an area where certain regulatory obligations are imposed. The Ministry of Finance in Mainland China has set up a China Internal Control Standards Committee. Additionally, the two major Mainland stock exchanges in Shanghai and Shenzhen issued guidelines for their listed companies in 2006. There are also a range of regulatory and listing requirements in the Hong Kong SAR relating to fraud control.

Internal controls are, however, also highly specialized systems requiring profession-al advice. Although standard procedures and guidelines exist, they will always need

---

25 Jones (2002), "A review of risk and the practical use of risk models by auditors, Internal control" Croner CCH, London, p.1-6.

26 PwC (2005), Global Economic Crime Survey 2005: Hong Kong, Hong Kong: PricewaterhouseCoopers.

27 See ICAC website at http://www.icac.org.hk/. Best Practice Packages can be downloaded. Also see the office of Pri-vacy Commissioner on Privacy (http://www.pco.org.hk) which provides comprehensive guidance on the monitoring of employees at work.

28 http://www.acfe.com and http://www.theiia.org/

to be tailored to the specific company and situation. In broad terms, the features of a good control scheme should be:

- Simple;
- Comprehensive;
- Verifiable;
- Properly resourced;
- Standardized on best practice;
- Equipped with IT support to minimize or eliminate poor practice;
- Able to influence change at the "working" level; and
- A system for monitoring operation of the internal controls.

As pointed out above, it should be a feature of a compliance culture that broad-based support and co-operation are given by all staff to the operation of such systems. That is why simplicity is so important. The systems should not be vulnerable to "expertise exclusivity" where access is limited to the few (sometimes only one) key employee(s) able to understand and operate the scheme.

The broad structure of a system of internal control includes:-

- Risk Management (proactive);
- Internal Control (general day-to-day control systems);
- Internal Control (specific IT controls); and
- Internal Audit (including spot-checks).

External Controls

External frauds are more difficult to detect. The approach to developing external controls will vary according to the kind of organisation and the external parties with which it deals. A "sampling and modelling" approach supplies a useful addition to specific systems developed to track transactions and money flow, all of which should comply with the same outline features described above for Internal Controls.

With sampling, specific transactions or activities are analysed on a random basis to check for fraud. Organizations must be aware of any change of circumstances that might affect the predicted results or indicate more useful target areas for sampling. The larger the sample size, the greater the cost but the more reliable the result is.

With modelling, organizations can form a view of expected levels of activity or through-put, and identify any unusual variations in these that might indicate fraud. For example, if procurement costs are unusually high, one might reasonably consider whether there is collusion between a purchasing officer and an external party to fix prices. Revenue collection is also a productive area where predicted and actual results can be compared.

IT issues

Over the last two decades, the single, simple development that has led to the rapid increase in fraud is the infiltration of the computer into almost all aspects of life and commerce. It is a technology that assists both the fraudsters and the prevention and detection of fraud. Some of the specific areas applying to fraud prevention are -

- Covert/continuous monitoring;
- E-mail audits and spot checks;
- Data mining (using programming to detect unusual activities or patterns); and
- Personal data protection and freedom of information legislative principles which define the limits of what can, and cannot, or should or should not, lawfully be done. It is necessary to obtain specific professional advice on the ambit of any scheme or intended action to ensure its legality. Some of these parametres will be addressed in the following chapter.

Chapter 6 – Detection

The concept of detection

The starting point of the detection of fraud must be the proper working of those systems that are put in place to prevent it, primarily internal but also external controls.

Acts of detection tend to be responses to a particular enquiry or alert that has been raised. They are therefore *reactive* events, while system controls will typically be *proactive* processes.

The first stage of detection has one objective - to determine whether a fraud may have been committed and needs to be investigated.

For example, a series of suspicious expense claims highlighted by internal controls or an audit of the process should be reviewed to determine whether they are fraudulent, or innocently explained. If the enquiry findings support the appearance of fraud, and in the absence of innocent explanations, one can say that a potential fraud has been "detected", which can then be investigated.

It is an important stage and a detection determination is not a decision to be taken lightly. Sensitivities about a fraud investigation are enormous, and regardless of the outcome of the investigation, its mere triggering will have its own indelible consequences and knock-on effects.

Before we look at the categories of detection, it is necessary to first consider the impact of the Personal Data (Privacy) Ordinance[29]. This Ordinance pertains to both the collection and use of information and relates to both the preceding and following chapters, as well as this one.

Personal Data (Privacy) Ordinance

To the extent that detection may generate information that falls within the broad legal definition of what constitutes "personal data", certain statutory controls concerning the way such data is collected, stored and used must be complied with. Subjects of an investigation maintain their own privacy rights for the information collected about them.

The controlling legislation for the Hong Kong SAR is the Personal Data (Privacy) Ordinance ("PD(P)O"). The policy of the Ordinance is set out in Schedule 1, but let

---

29 Cap 486, Laws of Hong Kong (www.hklii.org.hk).

us first consider s4 of the PD(P)O which prohibits the contravention of any of these principles:

"A data user shall not do an act, or engage in a practice, that contravenes a data protection principle unless the act or practice, as the case may be, is required or permitted under this Ordinance."

The six principles set out in Schedule 1 are -

DATA PROTECTION PRINCIPLES

Principle 1 - purpose and manner of collection of personal data

Principle 2 - accuracy and duration of retention of personal data

Principle 3 - use of personal data

Principle 4 - security of personal data

Principle 5 - information to be generally available

Principle 6 - access to personal data

The texts of Principles 1 and 3 are particularly relevant to our present context -

LAW CHECKLIST

Principle 1 - purpose and manner of collection of personal data

1. Personal data shall not be collected unless -
    - (a) the data are collected for a lawful purpose directly related to a function or activity of the data user who is to use the data;
    - (b) subject to paragraph (c), the collection of the data is necessary for or directly related to that purpose; and
    - (c) the data are adequate but not excessive in relation to that purpose.

2. Personal data shall be collected by means which are –
    a. lawful; and
    b. fair in the circumstances of the case.

3. Where the person from whom personal data are or are to be collected is the data subject, all practicable steps shall be taken to ensure that -
    - he is explicitly or implicitly informed, on or before collecting the data, of -
        - whether it is obligatory or voluntary for him to supply the data;
        - where it is obligatory for him to supply the data, the consequences for him if he fails to supply the data; and
    - he is explicitly informed –

- ◦ on or before collecting the data, of -
  - ◦ the purpose (in general or specific terms) for which the data are to be used; and
  - ◦ the classes of persons to whom the data may be transferred;
- ◦ on or before first use of the data for the purpose for which they were collected, of -
  - ◦ his rights to request access to and to request the correction of the data; and
  - ◦ the name and address of the individual to whom any such request may be made,

unless to comply with the provisions of this subsection would be likely to prejudice the purpose for which the data were collected and that purpose is specified in Part VIII of this Ordinance as a purpose in relation to which personal data are exempt from the provisions of data protection principle 6 (*Access to Personal Data*).

This connects to the section below, where certain activities, including investigation of unlawful or seriously improper behaviour, a criminal offence or a disciplinary offence, may be exempted from some, but not all of the data protection scheme.

LAW CHECKLIST

Principle 3 - use of personal data

- ■ Personal data shall not, without the prescribed consent of the data subject, be used for any purpose other than;
- ■ (a) the purpose for which the data were to be used at the time of the collection of the data; or
- ■ (b) a purpose directly related to the purpose referred to in paragraph (a).

To properly understand this, one should refer to the definitions set out in s2 of PD(P)O, the interpretation section, of which the followings are most applicable here -

- ■ "data" means any representation of information (including an expression of opinion) in any document, and includes a personal identifier;
- ■ "data subject" in relation to personal data, means the individual who is the subject of the data;
- ■ "data user" in relation to personal data, means a person who, either alone or jointly or in common with other persons, controls the collection, holding, processing or use of the data;
- ■ "disclosing" in relation to personal data, includes disclosing information inferred from the data;
- ■ "personal data" means any data -
  - ■ (a) relating directly or indirectly to a living individual;
  - ■ (b) from which it is practicable for the identity of the individual to be directly or indirectly ascertained; and
  - ■ (c) in a form in which access to or processing of the data is practicable;

- "use" in relation to personal data, including disclosing or transferring the data.

It is important to note the wide definition of personal data as including anything from which it is "practicable" to identify the data subject. Examples include a Hong Kong Identity Card Number and other personal identifiers such as a Hong Kong Driving License Number.

The scheme of the Ordinance is to set down the above set of principles and then provide for exceptions, or "exemptions", to them. These exemptions are related to any of the activities set out in Part VIII of the Ordinance, some of which are specified below, and all of which are potential grounds for avoiding the provisions of Data Protection Principles 3 and 6.

Applying these exemptions raises manyissues in practice. Of those set out in Part VIII of the Ordinance, perhaps the most important are those contained in s55 and s58, which provide for exemptions from the limitations of the Data Protection Principles in certain circumstances including when a crime or a disciplinary matter is under investigation, or to prevent crime or avoid financial loss. Section 55 first defines a broad range of circumstances where the exceptions may apply, and s58 is specifically targeted at "Crime, etc". For practical application, reference must be made to the specific wording:

LAW CHECKLIST

s55 Relevant Process

1. Personal data the subject of a relevant process are exempt from the provisions of data protection principle 6 and section 18(1)(b) until the completion of that process. (*the "relevant processes" are then defined in the following section*)
1. In this section –
   ◦ "completion" in relation to a relevant process, means the making of the determination concerned referred to in paragraph (a) of the definition of "relevant process";
   ◦ "relevant process" -
      ◦ (a) subject to paragraph (b), means any process whereby personal data are considered by one or more persons for the purpose of determining, or enabling there to be determined -
         ◦ (i) the suitability, eligibility or qualifications of the data subject for-
            + (A) employment or appointment to office;
            + (B) promotion in employment or office or continuance in employment or office;
            + (C) removal from employment or office; or
            + (D) the awarding of contracts, awards (including academic and professional qualifications), scholarships, honours or other benefits;
         ◦ (ii) whether any contract, award (including academic and

professional qualifications), scholarship, honour or benefit relating to the data subject should be continued, modified or cancelled; or
- (iii) whether any disciplinary action should be taken against the data subject for a breach of the terms of his employment or appointment to office.
- (b) does not include any such process where no appeal, whether under an Ordinance or otherwise, may be made against any such determination."

LAW CHECKLIST

s58 Crime, etc

1. Personal data held for the purposes of -
   a) the prevention or detection of crime;
   b) the apprehension, prosecution or detention of offenders;
   c) the assessment or collection of any tax or duty;
   d) the prevention, preclusion or remedying (including punishment) of unlawful or seriously improper conduct, or dishonesty or malpractice, by persons;
   e) the prevention or preclusion of significant financial loss arising from –
      - any imprudent business practices or activities of persons; or
      - unlawful or seriously improper conduct, or dishonesty or malpractice, by persons;
   f) ascertaining whether the character or activities of the data subject are likely to have a significantly adverse impact on any thing –
      - to which the discharge of statutory functions by the data user relates; or
      - which relates to the discharge of functions to which this paragraph applies by virtue of subsection (3); or
   g) discharging functions to which this paragraph applies by virtue of subsection (3) –
   h) are exempt from the provisions of data protection principle 6 and section 18(1) (b), where the application of those provisions to the data would be likely to –
      - prejudice any of the matters referred to in this subsection; or
      - directly or indirectly identify the person who is the source of the data.

2. (2) Personal data are exempt from the provisions of data protection principle 3 in any case in which –
   a) the use of the data is for any of the purposes referred to in subsection (1) (and whether or not the data are held for any of those purposes); and
   b) the application of those provisions in relation to such use would be likely to prejudice any of the matters referred to in that subsection,
      - and in any proceedings against any person for a contravention of any of those provisions it shall be a defence to show that he had reasonable grounds for believing that failure to so use the data would have been likely to prejudice any of those matters.

(3) ... [*(3), (4), (5) are provisions specific to financial regulators....*]

This provides a comprehensive scheme for which professional advice needs to be taken, particularly whenever -

1. There is a proposal to put in place a system that collects any kind of data that identifies people. This may include the use of security cameras in an office (or on a petrol station forecourt, for example), but will also be subject to the lightening of the burden under s35 of the PDPO, which makes allowances where there are repeated collections of data for the principles only to be complied with once in every 12-month period. For CCTV systems used solely for security purposes, the Commissioner has noted that although the system might be capable of identifying people, if that is not the use to which the system is put, the Ordinance is not engaged and no exemption is therefore required[30]. One important factor may be whether or not the images from the CCTV are recorded[31].

2. It is proposed to investigate, either overtly or covertly, an employee or a possible fraud and data are going to be collected or "used".

The Data User, i.e. the investigator, has to be careful and sensitive to the Data Subject's privacy rights. Any failure in this regard will often impair the investigation, lead to complaints and generally may be used by the defence (often unfairly) to undermine both the credibility and the professionalism of the investigators. This contributes to the potentially damaging impact of the fraud investigation itself.

The exemptions do not always apply. In 2005, an employer was not able to rely on them when it was found that the installation of 6 pinhole cameras in the working area of the Cheung Sha Wan Post Office breached the PDPO, even though the purpose was to investigate stamp thefts. Noting that one of the cameras had been placed on a corridor outside the female washrooms, Privacy Commissioner for Personal Data Woo concluded :

"The Commissioner was satisfied that Hongkong Post has a legitimate purpose to protect itself and its customers' property from theft and agreed that public confidence in mail security is of cardinal importance. However, in evaluating the extent of business risk of theft that it faced, the Commissioner looked at all the relevant circumstances and concluded that the evidence available did not show the existence of risk of loss to such extent as to justify the engaging in vast scale video monitoring activities, in particular the use of pinhole cameras which is highly privacy intrusive...Hongkong Post could not produce any documents, whether written or otherwise, evidencing the assessment process, if any, undertaken on the impact that such employee monitoring activities might have on employees' personal data privacy." [32]

It seems that it was, then, the extent of the invasive action combined with a failure to assess its likely impact that lay behind the Commissioner's critical findings.

---

30 See s35 of PDPO "Repeated collections of personal data in same circumstances".

31 See Case No 2001111 at http://www.pcpd.org.hk/.

32 See the Report # R05-7230 published under Section 48(2) of the PD(P)O on December 8, 2005.

There may well be surprise at the extent to which the apparently innocent collection of data may breach the PD(P)O. In another enquiry, for example, the Privacy Commissioner for Personal Data ("the Commissioner") cautioned as being unnecessary the collection of age and marital status from job applicants to an educational organisation unless it could be shown that it was necessary and not "excessive" within the meaning of the first data principle. It is useful to refer to the Commissioner's website which contains useful guidelines and codes of practice and online self-training together with case notes.

Internal Controls

Both internal and external controls combined with audits, comprise the first line of defence against fraud, and are part of the initial response to it. These measures are integral as much to the detection as they are to the prevention of fraud.

An organization's staff members are the key elements to both preventing and detecting fraud. This is seen on a day-to-day basis in their contributions to the operations of the systems of control.

System controls provide an opportunity for detection that -

- (i) exists at ground level, and is not reliant on expert or senior investigations;
- (ii) exists constantly (although the occasions of actual detection will each be unique events in themselves); and
- (iii) is independent of the audit and/or spot check.

There should, therefore, be systems for not only collecting and cross-checking the information gathered, but also for further considering improvements to the fraud detection performance.

Staff can contribute to a further level of risk assessment. In addition to the implementation of a control system by referring to a set of risks identified during the assessment, those who actually operate or comply with the systems on a daily basis will learn of additional particular risks that merit attention. There should be a system for recording these at "ground level" so that this piece of information is incorporated into the regular operation of the department, and into its prevention/detection systems.

Monitoring and Surveillance: Overt

Overt technology-based surveillance has become commonplace in modern life -

1. It is normal, for example, for networked terminals to be configured to raise an alert with the administrator if certain categories of websites are visited online;

2. Video and CCTV surveillance within the office areas and close adjoining proximities of the place of work is both common and accepted; and

3. Surveillance, in the form of record keeping, also occurs with use of personal electronic passes to enter and exit premises.

For fraud control, none of these forms of surveillance is likely to provide specific detection material, but all may be referred to at any stage of a fraud enquiry (including the detection phase), to provide back-up information about the general environment in which the fraud may have occurred.

However, the recording of information from these and other similar sources may engage the Personal Data (Privacy) Ordinance, if persons can be identified from the information. One must consider precisely what is recorded, and the way that information is then processed. In certain cases even the simplest of security objectives cannot be achieved if the information is not recorded. Strong arguments exist that this is a fundamental requirement for certain forms of CCTV surveillance and that it is an adequate and non-excessive measure for such cases.

In general, the data user will need to be able to justify the necessity of the data collection and recording which is not always possible to do. The Ordinance, therefore, can be seen to have direct impact on the levels of proactive security measures that are possible to install, in the absence of specific or repeated frauds, security breaches, or other preventable and serious losses that may justify an exemption.

Monitoring and Surveillance: Covert

The hazards of covert monitoring after the PD(P)O were highlighted in the previous section, when the Hongkong Post failed to establish an exemption for its use of 6 pinhole cameras to investigate stamp thefts. The only way for employers to be certain of the lawfulness of their proposed action is to engage the Personal Data Privacy Commissioner's enquiry process, which causes delay that may prove unacceptable in the context of an ongoing investigation.

A particular issue that may arise for others is the extent to which an organisation may secretly monitor employee communications within its departments, whether by e-mail or telephone. One must always refer to the requirement for "adequate but not excessive" measures set out in Data Protection Principle 1. [33]

It is hard to see how such uses can be justified for detection, since the existence of the fraud or crime that might justify such measures has yet to be confirmed together

---

[33] Case No 200507230 at www.pcpd.org.hk - It was held that principles 1(1) (excessive collection), 1(2) (collection by unfair means) and 5 (lack of transparent policy and practice) had been breached. The Hongkong Post Office was required to uninstall the pinhole cameras and to improve their policies and procedures on the monitoring of employees at work in accordance with the Ordinance.

with, more importantly, the identity of the suspect or suspects. Covert surveillance may be permissible in the context of an investigation of a detected fraud. A standard practice would be to consult professional opinion or the Commissioner's enquiries procedures, including the code of practices on monitoring of employees at work.

Non-systematic detection: spot-checks and whistle-blowers

By their nature, whistle-blower informants do not represent any part of systematic form of detection. In the same way, spot checks can be used to provide random reinforcement to system controls, introducing a highly unpredictable and cost-effective further element of both prevention, deterrence and, of course, detection.

The Fraud Detection Checklist

In addition to the topics covered above, the following areas of specific vulnerability should be considered as part of any review of a detection regime or spot check:

- "facilitation" and consultancy payments;
- whether purchase prices are in line with market rates;
- agents' success fees;
- unusual and/or one-off payments;
- charitable and political contributions;
- loans and exceptionally favourable or unusual credit terms;
- commissions and bonuses, both internal and external;
- bulk or repeated procurements;
- entertainment/personal expenses;
- 12th and 1st months in a financial year, generally;
- payroll;
- accounts receivable;
- bad debt provisions;
- offshore bank accounts; and
- use of offshore shell companies.

It should be reiterated that the essential purpose of the detection phase is to confirm the existence of a fraud or suspected fraud sufficient to merit further investigation. Upon confirmation, the relevant alerts can be raised and a formal investigation commences.

This formal investigation will seek to confirm or refute that conclusion by a structured and rigorous analysis of the evidence. That analysis, together with the structuring of the main investigation, is the subject of the following chapter.

Chapter 7 – Investigation Part 1 - Preliminary investigation

"Reasonable grounds to suspect"

The first stage of the investigation and the initial fact-finding exercise is completed at the end of the detection phase and leads to the conclusion that a fraud has or may have been committed, meriting further investigation. The enquiry then moves on to the preliminary investigation stage where the first critical investigator's task is to objectively confirm the basis of the "detection" conclusion. The investigator must challenge detection finding with this question: "Are there reasonable grounds to suspect that a fraud may have been committed?"

Although more formally framed, this amounts to a review of the detection stage. It is necessary because many (indeed most) frauds are initially detected by a staff member "on the ground" or a whistle-blower, not by professionally qualified investigators.

> *"Reasonable grounds": must be a set of facts or other indications that objectively appear to be reasonable. Although there may be a broad range of opinion, it must all be fact-based.*

The statutory language concerning the use of certain investigation powers uses the words "suspect", and "believe". The statutes also use phrasing that a fraud "may have been committed" and "has been committed". These fine distinctions are critical to a determination of whether each power may be engaged in a particular investigation, but for our purposes the internal investigator can disregard them. For determining whether to start an investigation it is sufficient to simply consider whether there exists "suspicion" that an offence "may have" been committed. "Reasonable suspicion" is not a hurdle that must be set particularly high. Law-makers do not mean to discourage reasonable investigations which, by definition, will often conclude that there is no fraud. Indeed there is no legislation, apart from the PD(P)O perhaps, to regulate the investigation of internal fraud by internal auditors or fraud investigators who are charged with the responsibilities of lawfully protecting company assets, preventing loss and recovering stolen property. Despite the lack of regulatory legislation, fraud investigators and internal auditors should still be extremely cautious when deciding to commence an investigation.

The existence of unexplained loss goes a long way towards establishing "reasonable suspicion".

The considered view is that a full-scale fraud inquiry must only be launched based upon proper grounds. It is not just a matter of the cost and disruption caused by a fraud inquiry. Reference has been made throughout this book to the special sensitivities associated with fraud offences. An investigator has a duty, professionally and ethically, to be acutely aware of the damage that simply launching a fraud investigation can inflict, regardless of the results of that investigation. There exists the danger to reputation of "guilt by association". This mainly affects three groups:

- First, obviously, the individuals that are suspected. It should be noted that anyone questioned or investigated *might* be considered a suspect;
- Second, those people whose workplace failures or omissions might be considered to have facilitated the fraud, or those who have a specific duty to prevent it; and
- Third, the commercial reputation of a company where fraud is investigated. Companies, their customers and the public will tend to perceive a fraud investigation as a negative attribute. It undermines the trust and confidence that support commercial reputations and relationships, and also creates concerns about the safety of money and value-flow through the organization.

Only after considering all these factors should a fraud investigation be *commenced* and *pursued.* Careful, objective consideration and thorough testing must be applied to the initial report that a fraud has been detected.

"Think like a judge"

To answer the "reasonable grounds to suspect" question, think like a judge. This means three things:

A. Know the law;

B. Investigate the facts; and

C. Only draw conclusions that are supported by the evidence.

A. Know the law The law must form the framework of an enquiry. It is for this reason that this book includes a full "map" of the applicable laws. Because it is not possible at the initial stage of the investigation to confine an enquiry to an exact charge or civil claim, the investigator must be constantly considering the full spectrum of potential charges and damages claims so they can decide which ones might apply within the broad range of applicable law. That is why the investigator must know all of the laws, at least in their headline form.

It is only a dishonest lawyer who says he carries the entire works of Archbold[34] in his mind. Law is not a memory test; it is a skill and a science - the skill of knowing where to look for the precise details of the relevant law, and the science of beginning with the legal questions and then testing facts against them to establish what they do and do not prove.

---

34 Said to be the most comprehensive reference book for practising criminal lawyers in Hong Kong.

B. Investigate the facts In law, a fact is either something that is admitted or which can be proved. The law precisely informs us what needs to be proven (the discrete elements of the offence or the components of the tort, etc.). One must then analyse the evidence to see if it offers sufficient facts to prove those elements. The process is to identify, collect and organize factual information to decide whether there are valid legal conclusions that can be drawn, namely, whether there exists a provable charge, damages claim, or accusation of misconduct.

At the initial stage the facts may be limited to those in the initial detection report. It is necessary to consider whether and how, the facts alleged can be proved *with admissible evidence.*

C. Only draw conclusions that are supported by the evidence. The facts must then be matched with the relevant laws to determine the appropriate charge, claim or complaint. At this early stage, conclusions will be provisional, and it is acceptable, indeed preferable, if they identify only a broad range of enquiry or potential charges and complaints. Several alternatives should be considered at this stage.

Clients (fraud victims) tend to not like this. Clients and bosses prefer simple clear answers. It's required to be vigilant however, and to be careful not to allow top-down pressures to narrow or over-simplify the enquiry at this early stage. Senior corporate officers may need to be told what they don't want to hear – that there is a range of possibilities and further, typically urgent, enquiries must be made.

By way of example, a preliminary enquiry might proceed on the basis of this detection report which has been redacted from an actual case to protect anonymity -

> *"During a recent on-site review, information was uncovered suggesting that certain customary business practices might contravene X Company's policy, and be illegal under recent legislation. You have been engaged to investigate potentially improper conduct and to determine whether company policy or the law have been violated by the payments to government official, Mr. Z, that were authorized by company director, Mr. Y."*

The focus of enquiry may shift fairly quickly and broadly in these early stages. It seems to be an enquiry into possible corruption, but if Mr. Y had a share in any of the money paid to Mr. Z, then fraud becomes a possibility. In both instances, there may be a conspiracy. Or, it may be simply that what emerges is nothing more than a breach of company policy warranting only a disciplinary proceeding. Then again, it is possible that the whole matter can be satisfactorily explained, and that nothing untoward has happened.

Even at this early stage, you should keep in mind *admissibility* of evidence, as this will relate to the way an investigator questions people and to decisions of whether to caution them or not, should criminal charges be a possibility. For example, a statement from Mr. Y's wife that Mr. Y and Mr. Z were engaged in a conspiracy, the investigator must also be aware that it is not possible to compel a wife to testify against her husband[35]. Matters of law and evidence make a difference at these early stages, and continue to provide the framework for an enquiry because they define what must be proven and the evidential requirements that must ultimately be met.

If an investigator decides based on his review of the evidence that, in confirmation of the detection report, there are reasonable grounds to suspect that a fraudulent or corrupt act may have been committed then it will be reasonable to proceed with the full investigation. In the above example, it would probably be enough to identify the existence of the personal payment to a government official, a breach of company policy, or both, in order to create a reasonable basis for suspicion that fraud or a discipline-worthy transgression may have occurred.

Having drawn that conclusion, and *without necessarily deciding* a full inquiry be launched, the next, and equally important, job for the investigator is to locate and, if possible, initiate all possible channels of asset recovery. Time is very much of the essence for asset recovery, as indeed it is for the collection and preservation of evidence. It should be noted that in the above example, it may be inappropriate to initiate an early stage asset recovery process.

Asset recovery

For the corruption offences that are covered by the Prevention of Bribery Ordinance, a helpful regime exists in sections 14C-E[36]. The Court may grant orders restraining the disposal of identified assets, but only to, or on behalf of, the Commissioner of the ICAC. This power can be exercised against any person that is the "subject of an investigation" for an offence under that Ordinance, however, it is likely that once misappropriated assets have been identified for a suspected bribery offence, such an investigation will have been initiated. To this extent, the power is a useful one where bribery is suspected, even though bribery is outside the purview of this book.

The powers granted by section 15 of the Organised and Serious Crimes Ordinance[37] are of limited value here. These can only be used for "realizable property" and on application by the prosecutor of an offence, and are therefore unlikely to be engaged in the early stages of an investigation. However, fraud *is* included in the list of crimes covered by these powers (as listed in section 12 of Schedule 1

---

35 This relates to the "compellability" of the wife. An investigator also needs to consider, for example, whether a proposed witness is legally "competent" to testify, or may be excluded on the grounds of disability such as mental health grounds, including depression or stress.

36 Prevention of Bribery Ordinance (Cap 201).

37 Organized and Serious Crimes Ordinance (Cap 455).

of the Organized and Serious Crimes Ordinance), but the provisions can only be engaged in cases where the value of the criminal proceeds is HK$100,000 or more and criminal proceedings have been commenced or are soon to come.

Because of the above limitations, two other methods of asset recovery should be considered in the early stages:

1. Confrontation - It is a significant mitigation when a suspect makes early and complete restitution of the proceeds of his or her wrong doing. Confronting those involved with this suggestion becomes an available option, but this step is a risky one. Depending on the situation and person concerned, it must be carefully considered whether confrontation is likely to lead to the preservation and recovery or to the dispersal of the assets in question. Also, a decision to confront must take into account the severity of the offence and the damage to reputation that may be caused. Any decision to confront must receive the highest level of authorization, and then only with appropriate legal advice, because the ultimate decision about what level of disclosure to make is a matter of the highest sensitivity.

2. *"Mareva"*[38] *and other injunctions*: Civil powers to freeze real property assets held by a third party such as a bank exist, and their use can also be considered, whatever the nature of the fraud and no matter whether it is likely to lead to disciplinary, civil or criminal proceedings. The flexibility of these common law remedies makes them the first choice for asset recovery for many investigators.

The Fraud Investigation Checklist

Once the preliminary matters have been addressed and the decision to launch a full investigation has been made, the fraud checklist is completed so that a full-scale formal investigation can be initiated. This is the final, preliminary matter that signals the launch of the full-scale investigation. A checklist should set down, in outline, a broad agenda for an enquiry. In doing so, the fraud investigator should not be distracted from the essential flexibility and availability for tangential thought that will remain essential throughout the investigation. The checklist must not become the tail that wags the dog.

---

38 A jurisdiction at common law, but actually an equitable remedy, exists to freeze assets, but only where it can be shown that there is a likelihood of them being removed from the jurisdiction. A large body of law exists on the application in practice of the rules identified in the leading case of Mareva Companiera Naviera SA v International Bulk Carriers SA (1975) 2 Lloyd's Rep 509. For a recent application, and for an example of the preparedness of common law courts to assist globally, see Cinar Corporation & others v Hasanain Panju [2006] EWHC 2557 (QB,) where it was appropriate to make a worldwide freezing order against the assets of the defendant, who faced compelling allegations of a substantial fraud. Although proceedings were initiated in Canada, the UK Courts were prepared to make the order. Oppenshaw J spoke of a "clear and compelling interest that attempts by foreign courts to identify, to freeze and, in the event of Judgment in due course, to recover the proceeds of fraud on this scale are not frustrated by flight, or by the movement of persons and their assets from one country to another."

Broadly, a fraud investigation checklist should be a substantial document that identifies, as exhaustively as possible, all relevant topics these following headings together with any others that might be relevant to a specific investigation.

Chart 15 FRAUD INVESTIGATION CHECKLIST

ITEM	REMARKS
Consideration of detection report.	
"Reasonable grounds to suspect"?	
Asset recovery	
Management notified?	
Consider whether to notify Police/ICAC/ Regulators.	
Damage limitation, crisis management. Any publicity issues?	
Review any applicable internal policies or procedures.	
Create initial time-line of reported events.	
Immediate witnesses interviewed?	
Documents or any other relevant evidence preserved?	
IT – what computers/data storage media are involved. Can these be seized/subject to data recovery?	
Early site visit where relevant.	
Other relevant third parties identified, contacted?	
Analysis of what is known so far about general connections/links analysis, internal and external.	
Any relevant errors, mistakes or gaps in procedures, policies or internal controls requiring immediate remedy?	
List of potential legal/disciplinary charges, the components of each, and how each component is to be proved.	
Independent legal advice required at this stage?	

Set a date for preliminary written report to management. At this stage, the investigator should also be prepared to give indications about (i) budget costs of the investigation (ii) any data protection or privacy issues.	
Investigation plan in outline, comprising:- • *List of witnesses to interview.* • *Interview approaches for each.* • *Investigative strategies for different areas of investigation – i.e. Covert/Overt etc?* • *Identification and confirmation of how to prove: (i) intention (ii) causation.* • *Detailed review of all financial documentation.* • *Decision whether to retain independent financial/ legal/other expert advice?* • *Detailed financial and documentary analysis with conclusions.* • *Background/ID/Asset checks on participants? Court records, public documents, credit reference agencies, internet searches etc.* • *Witness statements in proper form, admissible, and signed. Have attachments and appendices been properly prepared?* • *Review of all evidence and final forensic analysis against potential charges, allegations, etc.*	
Check time-line against investigation plan including dates for both preliminary and final written reports and their submission to relevant superior/client.	

As with any *pro forma* list, each entry is capable of leading to its own internal set of further questions. Equally, other issues that need to be included but are not shown here may arise. No generic checklist can be exhaustive. What is offered here should ensure a thorough pre-investigation "audit" and provide a structural starting point. From this, the investigator should develop, on a case-by-case basis, the necessary strategy and methodology for each matter that will include both modifications to the checklist and, on occasion, the development of a completely unique checklist.

On full completion of the checklist, the investigation is ready to move on to the "action level".

The Association of Certified Fraud Examiners also issues similar checklists for fraud investigations which can be accessed and downloaded at:

http://www.acfe.com/documents/managing-business-risk.pdf.

Chapter 8 – Investigation Part 2 - Gathering the evidence

Two levels of concealment

At this juncture we note again the secret and hidden nature of fraud that is its defining characteristic. The investigator must remain aware of this because it means that what is being investigated is packaged in not one but two levels of concealment[39]. These are:

- Concealment of the occurrence of the crime; and
- Concealment as an actual part of the way that the crime is committed.

Investigating fraud is not the same as investigating an incident such as a workplace accident, an auto collision, or a crime, such as theft or robbery, where the victim and the occurrence of the event will usually be obvious. These incidents may also include a level of concealment – the accident may involve deliberately concealed or simply latent features that need to be uncovered or discovered, and the "obvious" crime will still usually involve at least an element of concealment of the identity of the perpetrator with perhaps some attempt to conceal the occurrence. This concealment of the crime is, in a sense, only to be expected.

With fraud and corruption we must add a second level of concealment that reflects the essential element of the acts – their deception. This involves the perpetrator's deliberate attempts, as part of the scheme itself, to conceal every feature of the event and, in particular, even its occurrence. These may include deceptions such as falsification, destruction or removal of key documents, etc. In incidences of corruption, there is not necessarily an obvious victim. This explains why it is so difficult to estimate the incidence levels of fraud and corruption. We can only talk about detected acts of fraud and corruption. Undetected acts are impossible to count.

It is in this environment of "double concealment" that the fraud investigator works. And so we must add another list of three factors that an investigator must remember at all times:

We have already mentioned the time-line in the fraud checklist, and will show in the following section on report writing how that evidence is best presented in linear form, chronologically and with a narrative style.

---

39 "Specific corrupt acts are inherently difficult to detect let alone prove in the normal way", per Bokhary JA in Attorney General v Hui Kin-hong [1995] 1 HKCLR 227 at 235, line 33.

But that is not how the investigator should always work. The construction of a time-line is an essential part of the investigation mainly because evidence is usually created over time. Perpetrators of fraud and corruption know that linear thinking governs us, which is exactly why the investigator must not be confined by this longitudinal approach. It is necessary for the investigator to look both laterally, across different fields of apparently unconnected groups of evidence, as well as vertically, at different levels of the process or related processes, as well as tangentially. While the investigator's method is perhaps their greatest strength, it can also be a weakness if not combined with the ability to think multi-dimensionally.

For example, many frauds happen across the year-end divide, with one payment at the end of one financial year, followed by a second payment at the beginning of the following year. The fraudster is aware that many of us will think in "financial years" and uses that pattern of thinking to conceal the fraud, by dividing relevant transactions between the years, so as to help to conceal their connection.

Powers of Investigation under the Independent Commission Against Corruption Ordinance, the Prevention of Bribery Ordinance and the Organized and Serious Crimes Ordinance

Data Protection issues apply as much to the process of investigation as they do to the processes of prevention and detection. When an investigator gathers information about people, their data privacy rights must be respected. The 6 Data Protection Principles must be abided and any investigation conducted in full compliance with the company's Code of Conduct on Monitoring of Employees at the workplace.

Hong Kong has recognized that the difficulties detecting and investigating fraud and corruption do require some special powers for investigation authorities. As a matter of policy, the approach in Hong Kong is that special investigative and enforcement powers relating to corruption offences are vested in the Commissioner of the Independent Commission Against Corruption. The Commissioner of Police is also empowered under various ordinances to investigate fraud related serious crimes.

It is a professional mandate that an investigator should always be aware and mindful of the legal limits of his powers. Unlawfully gathered evidence is frequently inadmissible in disciplinary or court proceedings. Conversely, it would be wrong for an investigator to fail to deploy an investigative tool or simply through ignorance of its existence and availability.

Powers change as laws and regulations are made and amended, and keeping fully up-to-date must also be regarded as a professional requirement.

Independent Commission Against Corruption Ordinance (Cap 204)

While the Independent Commission Against Corruption Ordinance generally pertains only to the Commissioner of the ICAC's powers of investigation, and is not, therefore, the subject of this book, there is an important power under Section 13(1)(d) of that Ordinance that offers wider application. This is the Commissioner's ability to delegate his power to others, specifically to:

> *"(d) authorize in writing any person to perform any of his duties and to exercise such powers under this Ordinance and the Prevention of Bribery Ordinance (Cap 201) as he may specify. (Amended 10 of 2000 s. 47)"*

It should first be noted that the power to delegate applies both to this Ordinance and the Commissioner's powers under the Prevention of Bribery Ordinance.

The Commissioner's delegable powers under Section 13 of the Ordinance primarily relate to his access to government and public documents. These may be useful to an enquiry such as the example given above, where a company has internally identified that one of its employees has been making payments to a government official.

Where the power is delegated, so also by s44(2) of the Interpretation and General Clauses Ordinance (cap 1)[40] will be any duty incidental thereto or rationally and fairly in a public law sense, and to be reasonably satisfied in relation to the suspicion or belief that a bribery offence has or may have been committed, as the case may be.

While the Commissioner's decision to delegate and allow others to act on his or her behalf will always be his or her own, one may approach him or her for the purposes. Delegation powers provide the Commissioner with an ability to relieve the pressure on his or her own resources, and take quick, limited action through a delegate investigator before reaching a decision whether to initiate an ICAC investigation. It may be, however, that a company would not choose to make such an application, for many different reasons. In each case, specific legal advice will be required as to the delegation, its feasibility, and what precisely it might entail.

Prevention of Bribery Ordinance (Cap 201)

The special investigative powers available under the Prevention of Bribery Ordinance (POBO), which as stated above are delegable[41] include:

---

40 s44(2) Interpretation and General Clauses Ordinance (Cap 1).

41 See also s2(1) of the Prevention of Bribery Ordinance which defines "investigating officer" as " any person authorized by the Commissioner to exercise the powers of an investigating officer under this Ordinance".

s 13 Special powers of investigation;

s 13A Order to make material available and to render assistance;

s 13B Disclosure of information obtained under section 13A;

s 13C Restriction on publication of information disclosed under section 13B;

s 14 Power to obtain information;

s 16 Power to obtain assistance;

s 17 Further powers of search; and

s 17A-C Travel documents.

The power in s13 involves the right to inspect "any share account, purchase account, club account, subscription account, investment account, trust account, mutual or trust fund account, expense account, bank account or other account of whatsoever kind or description, and any banker's books, company books, documents or other article of or relating to any person named or otherwise identified in writing by the Commissioner" and "likely to be relevant for the purposes of an investigation of" an offence under POBO. Essentially it is a power to inspect and copy any document likely to be relevant to the enquiry. This is supported both by the additional powers in sections 13A-C, which are designed to give access to otherwise confidential tax records, and the power to require information under Section14.

The power under Section 13 of the POBO is exercisable by the Commissioner and is in itself binding on all persons, except in the case where its use involves an order for compliance against a suspect, when an *ex parte* application to Hong Kong's Court of First Instance must be made first. The construction of this power in this way means that it can be used covertly, if necessary, before confronting the suspect.

Other than under Section 13 and Section 16 (below), the powers under POBO mentioned above are only exercisable on application, which may be made *ex parte*, to the Court of First Instance.

The remainder of the scheme contains powers to require assistance of any public servant (s16), exercisable by any "investigation officer", and powers to apply to the Court for search warrants (s17) and for the detention of travel documents (s17A-C9).

Other POBO powers that should be mentioned are not strictly investigative. Those relating to evidence will be dealt with in Chapter 9, but three are worthy of special mention here.

The first two of these somewhat unusual powers reside in ss22-3 of the POBO, and include aspects of Hong Kong's UK common law history, but are more resonant of US legal policy, to make deals with offenders, in order to be able to obtain evidence from the more minor players and accomplices to secure the conviction of the main culprits in the fraud. The first of these, s22, provides that the giving or receipt of a bribe is not in itself, without more, enough to establish that a person is an accomplice to the crime. The second, in s23, enables the court "at the request in writing of the Secretary for Justice" to provide a person with immunity from prosecution in exchange for his evidence. The details of these powers are highly specific, and professional legal advice obviously is required for their use, but their existence is an important part of the POBO that investigators should be aware of.

These are important provisions to protect accomplices from conviction, which may improve investigators' access to their useful evidence. They are to some extent reinforced by the terms of s60 of the Criminal Procedure Ordinance whereby it is no longer required for a judge to warn against the dangers of convicting an accused on the basis of evidence from an alleged accomplice.

In practice this means that if a person has accepted or given a bribe but there is no other evidence against him, (i) that evidence alone is not enough to establish that person's guilt as an accomplice, and, (ii) in Court the simple, uncontroverted defence allegation of the accused, that a person giving evidence for the prosecution is an accomplice, will not by itself undermine the alleged accomplice's evidence making it necessary for the judge to give the jury a warning about its validity.

These provisions are further supplemented by the important provisions of s30A of the POBO, which provide informers with protection against disclosure of their identity, except in the situation where the Court is satisfied that that informer's evidence is false[42].

Another POBO provision worth mentioning is s29, which provides that anyone making a false report or misleading an investigating officer authorized by the Commissioner under s13 of the POBO, is committing an offence punishable by a fine of up to HK$20,000 and imprisonment of up to one year.

Organized and Serious Crimes Ordinance

This Ordinance sets out a potent scheme designed to assist in the investigation of organized crime[43] which includes:

s 3 Requirement to furnish information or produce material;

s 4 Order to make material available;

---

42 s30A Prevention of Bribery Ordinance (Cap 201).

43 See Organised and Serious Crimes Ordinance (Cap 455) ss 3 – 7.

s 5 Authority for search;

s 6 Disclosure of information obtained under section 3, 4 or 5; and

s 7 Offence of prejudicing investigation.

The scheme is engaged by application to the Court, either by the Secretary of Justice or an "authorized officer". Under s2(1) of the Ordinance, the designation of an "authorized" officer is interpreted fairly strictly, meaning either a Police Officer, a Customs Officer or "any other person authorized in writing by the Secretary for Justice for the purposes of this Ordinance."

Legal Professional Privilege

The investigator needs to master two principal areas of academic expertise. The first is the law relating to the area of operations in which he or she is working, including both the relevant criminal and civil law. The second area is the law of evidence in both the civil and the criminal arenas.

These core subjects require specific study, and will not even be summarized here. One particular issue of the law of evidence does merit discussion, that being the Legal Professional Privilege. This, along with the Caution (discussed in the final section of this chapter), can critically affect whether evidence is admissible in court.

Most forms of privilege exist in order to protect from disclosure in court certain kinds of information for public policy reasons, including fairness. The Legal Professional Privilege is one of these. It shields communications between a lawyer and his client from disclosure in court. The policy rationale is to promote an effective and fair system of justice where a client can communicate candidly and confidentially with his lawyer. These communications are inherently protected, and no particular claim for privilege needs to be logged. They are protected from disclosure in court the moment they happen. The Privilege extends to all communications, in whatever form and can reach beyond the Lawyer-Client relationship to include others with whom they interact such as, in specified conditions, expert witnesses or expert consultants, such as computer forensic specialists or certified fraud examiners, instructed by a lawyer to undertake specific tasks.

This means that an internal investigator must not collect information which will be protected by this important Common Law privilege. An investigator should immediately seek professional legal advice regarding the proper retention and disclosure of lawyer-client communications in the event that this type of information was collected during the course of a routine monitoring of staff communications such as by recorded telephone conversations or email exchanges.

Although certain exceptions exist, these exceptions are not presented here as this topic merits a separate and specialized study by a student investigator.

Site Visit

The first site visit should take place as soon as possible after the reported event. This is critical. Evidence can quickly deteriorate and dissipate. Depending on whether the investigation is overt or not at that stage, carefully consider whether this should be an unannounced visit or a visit by appointment. In most cases, an unannounced visit is preferable. Depending on the situation, the investigator should take business cards to enable potential witnesses to conveniently contact them. It seems obvious, but bears mentioning - don't forget a notebook and pen! Also, remember that the notebook itself may need to be submitted as evidence, so its contents should be professionally recorded which entails:

- Acquiring a preferably hard-backed notebook with printed, sequentially numbered pages; and
- Indicating times in a 24-hour format (i.e. 14.22 for 22 minutes past 2 p.m.) noted as each new entry is made, as well as time and date of arrival and departure at the site.

At the first site visit your objectives are to:

- Establish the accuracy of the "detection" report that has been provided;
- Establish a sequence of events;
- Locate evidence, or where it might have been moved to, or to determine if it has been destroyed and then to seek either to recover or preserve it;
- Establish a list of potential witnesses;
- Identify, if any, the potential suspects; and
- Be alert to any possibility of asset recovery or preservation/protection.

All of these objectives are subject to the investigator's instinct and judgment about the extent to which his or her efforts may be counter-productive by leading to the concealment or destruction of evidence and assets, or by discouraging co-operation from witnesses, or alerting potential suspects. These are judgments better made with experience.

Other Equipment: The investigator should take an audio recorder of some kind. All interviews should be recorded and the time and date of the recording written on the disc or tape, as well as spoken into the recorded interview. Also take a digital camera as photographic evidence, where appropriate. It is typically the most powerful in court.

For instance, a photographic image of the screen of a computer under examination will be extremely useful to identify if any unlawful transactions have taken place. Remember not to turn off the computer as valuable information may be lost once the computer is switched off. A computer with suspected evidence should be put under guard pending a forensic examination by computer experts.

It is important to register a time and date on each photograph or video image.

Gloves and plastic bags for containing evidence should be brought along, together with tweezers for certain kinds of investigation, and disposable gloves for any occasion where evidence will be handled.

Additionally, an investigator should bring both recordable CDs and a large capacity portable disc drive for downloading and copying digital data. An investigator may consider learning how to use other software tools, including data recovery programs, and keeping them available, but these also may be appropriately administered by an independent expert.

Interviews (1): Objectives, Strategies and Skill Sets

What are interviews? In many circumstances, one thinks of the classic TV interview as a "2-on-1" meeting in which the interview subject is outnumbered. That is not normally the case for the fraud investigator, who will conduct many of his interviews "1-on-1". Human dynamics come strongly into play with that ratio.

Objectives

> *The interviewer's objectives:* The overall objective of any interview is simply stated – GET TO THE TRUTH. But that is not always possible to achieve in a simple, or even single, stage.

In this context, don't forget that the most powerful form of evidence in any proceeding is the admission. That is, **the *admissible* and *provable* admission**. While an interview has many different purposes, this is undoubtedly the primary objective, and it is one of which the interview subject will be unaware of. In achieving this objective, the investigator/interviewer will bear in mind the important secondary objective, which is that an admission can only be obtained with interviewee compliance, even in a case of torture (which we are not suggesting here!). The very nature of an admission or confession is that it is given by the witness's own free will.

Beyond this, obviously there is a whole array of objectives concerning the detection and investigation of an incident and the collection of evidence. These are summarized in the Fraud Checklist at the end of Chapter 7. Most of them should have already been considered by the investigator before the interview stage. Particularly:

- It is important at an early stage to preserve evidence, so one of the top priorities is to discover what that evidence is, where it might be located, and then to take necessary steps to remove, copy or otherwise preserve it;

- Issues of asset recovery will also be on the investigator's mind at this stage as well; and
- The investigator should compile a primary list of the people involved.

The interview subject's objectives: Interview subject's objectives will differ hugely depending on whether he is guilty, innocent or uncertain about whether he may be implicated. The objective of the guilty party will be primarily concealment (to protect the fraud or corrupt act) and, if that fails, probably denial. The innocent interviewee will usually have a primary objective of disassociating himself from the corrupt or fraudulent act, if he knows about it. Even an innocent individual may still present as circumspect or inhibited if he has concern that he may be erroneously implicated in misconduct. Accordingly an investigator should be aware that some measure of avoidance, and even sometimes a dishonest response may come from an innocent interviewee. It is an interviewer's task to clear up ambiguity and misconceptions that may inhibit or prevent full disclosure from an innocent witness.

For example, if there are elements of bribery, perhaps by way of the payment of a "commission", there are provisions within the Prevention of Bribery Ordinance (POBO) that may assist in obtaining witness compliance -

- Section 22 of the POBO provides that the receiver or giver of a bribe will not be regarded as an accomplice to the illegal activity, if there is no more than only proof of that payment. The word "only" is important in emphasizing there must be no unlawful circumstances apart from the existence of the transaction itself;
- Section 30 of the POBO prohibits the disclosure of the identity of a person under investigation under this act, and of the details of the investigation; and
- Section 30A of the POBO protects informers, as long as their evidence is not intentionally false.

The prosecution may also offer an accomplice who has actually committed illegal acts immunity from prosecution.

All of these are tools in the public investigator's armory, but obviously not all are available to the private investigator, particularly the power to grant immunities. Depending on the perceived objectives of the interviewee, the interviewer will need to be alert to respond in the way that optimizes the way the interview is structured and carried out, and also to determine the best timing for when to interview and when not to.

Strategies and Skill Sets

Set out below are some bullet points relating to these issues, primarily connected to the question of "What is the skill set needed to achieve this strategic objective"? It is suggested the novice investigator should pause with each to consider the personal preparations and skills he needs to acquire to move comfortably through the following scenarios.

Preliminarily - Interviewing is a complex dynamic.

Nature of the interview

- It involves people communicating;
- It involves trying to make something happen;
- Accomplish a goal; and
- Get from point A to point B.

Preparation for the interview

- The interviewer interprets the progress of the interview and interviewee's responses through verbal, vocal and non-verbal behaviour;
- Identify the specific skills required in order to conduct the interview;
- Establish the goal of the interview;
- Establish what facts are available regarding the investigation;
- Establish what facts are available regarding the interviewee; and
- Be aware of (i) the interviewer's and (ii) the interviewee's own strengths and weaknesses. These include responses to potential stressors (discomfort with anger, or a propensity to get angry) as well as, perhaps, less expert knowledge than the interviewee's on a core issue.

Conduct of the Interview - (1) Evaluate (2) Control (3) Modify

At the commencement of the interview, the interviewer explains the reasons, exhibits, formality of written statements and the consequences of fabricating answers, etc.

During the interview, obtain the interviewee's own account without prompting, interruption or challenging. Before the closure, aim for mutual understanding and facilitate the development of a positive attitude. It is recommended a three-step approach be used to achieve this.

1. Evaluate

Is the interviewee truthful or deceptive?

During the interview, determine when the interviewee is truthful and when deceptive.

2. Control

During the interview process, power or control is demonstrated by the ability to elicit an intended response. Endeavour to cause behaviour of the interviewee to reach a level wherein the interviewer can begin to make some evaluation of the interviewee.

3. Modify

Before the interviewer can change the behaviour of the interviewee from an unproductive level to a productive level, he may need to change or modify his approach. This may then be reflected in a modification of the interviewee's response. Such "mirrored" behaviour can only happen where there is a relationship established between the persons concerned.

The interviewer tests to see if this is happening by crossing or uncrossing his legs, or even by the classic example of lighting (and offering) a cigarette, to see if the behaviour is copied.

The objective is, of course, witness compliance.

Some of the skills needed by an interviewer

Data collection –

- Ability to detect deception;
- Admission-seeking (persuasive) powers;
- An ability to control temper together with a natural sense of empathy (for empathy, see further below); and
- An ability to understand and interpret non-verbal communication.

Dealing with an interviewee strategy - deception by omission

NOTE – deception by omission is not as noticeable to the non-attentive eye and ear. But it is much easier to leave out (to omit) a psychologically threatening truth than it is to insert deceptive information into the narrative (to lie). To the deceiver, omission is not the same as lying. But to the interviewer, both indicate the same thing and have the same result in obscuring the true facts of the situation.

- If deception is the interviewee's objective, the behaviour, verbal and non-verbal, is directed towards the accomplishment of this objective;
- If the truth is the interviewee's goal then behaviour tailored to that end is employed (see further); and
- Look for changes in behaviour and explore those areas;

And remember -

- Deception by omission is usually the first tactical choice of the deceiver;

- The deceiver chooses to leave out the relevant information;
- Place questions in areas indicated by behaviour changes suggestive of omission; and
- Try to move the deceiver from an omission strategy into the necessity of positive deception of commission of the offence – i.e. from negative omission to positive lying.

Some signs of deception by omission -

- These may be verbal or non-verbal, relating to the voice, the body, or a manner of behaviour; including:
    - Stalling;
    - Vouching for his/her own veracity; and
    - Avoiding eye contact (but note cultural differences – for some this is simply a sign of respect).

Some tips on empathy:

Three tips for improving the "empathy of the communication":

1. Always try to sit at the same level as the other(s). Being below subliminally registers as being weak. The one in the non-dominant position may over-compensate for this by being aggressive.

2. A short-cut to a sense of rapport is to match the other person's body signs, even if they are neutral or negative. This may have a positive effect – i.e., a non-verbal "I know how you feel/You know how I feel" response[44]. It can also be taken to absurd levels of almost comic parody. Be sane and subtle.

3. Don't forget to smile. Not over-smile. But smile, particularly when dealing with specific cultural backgrounds, e.g. Caucasians.

As already mentioned, the interviewer requires various skills. While some skills are equally important, two in particular are discussed below because they are areas where the expertise is less likely to be shared by the interview subject and therefore areas where particularly advantage may be gained by the interviewer.

---

44 See Eaton and Johnson: "Communicate with Emotional Intelligence" p66 ('How To' books, 2001).

Interviews (2): Questioning

Questions are the stock-in-trade of the interviewer.

Open Questions:

"Tell me what happened."

This question seeks to exert no control over the interview subject and is a simple request for information. The interviewer is asking the witness for his or her own version of events, and may need to remind the witness to confine the information to what he or she actually saw, heard, or knew, as opposed to what has been reported or passed on by others. Open questions are not usually based on any knowledge that the interviewer may or may not have. The answer is completely up to the witness. Such questions activate the interviewee's thinking process and may promote a more protracted response.

Closed or Leading Questions:

"It's true that you were the last person to leave the office on that day, isn't it?"

These questions seek to control the witness, and instead of seeking information, they are seeking confirmation or admission of information the interviewer already holds. The question contains information to which the answer "Yes" or "No" is invited. When the answer is something else, the familiar admonishment, "Answer the question, 'Yes' or 'No'" will be used if the interviewer has decided to deploy some aggression. The use of these questions will exert pressure on a witness, and will not elicit new information, but just substantiate what is already known. These also take the risk of revealing what you know. If the information is known by the interviewer, but denied by the witness, clear signs of the guilty witness will begin to emerge.

Piggy-Backing (Also known as "Echo Return"):

"I last saw her yesterday"

"So when you saw her yesterday, what was she wearing?"

Piggy-backing is a technique that establishes an interviewer's control over the witness in a subtle way, but with real benefits of building a sense of relationship, and of "common story telling". If a third party is also listening to the interview, it clarifies the narrative in that person's mind. It simply involves using information from the last part of the interview subject's answer to form the beginning of the next question. It is like a "domino effect", creating a series of narrative links between the questions and answers to form them into a more unified piece of evidence as a whole.

Remember -

- Questions are excellent tools to control the thinking of others. They can also be used actually to impart information.
- Questioning allows the interviewer to utilize the interviewee's inclination to talk. When someone is asked a question there is a natural inclination to answer.
- Extend common courtesy (e.g. shake hands).
    - Is the interviewee willing, reluctant or refusing to engage this basic social act?
    - Is the interviewee's hand dry or moist?
    - Is the muscle tone of the interviewee tight and tense or fluid and relaxed?

The interviewer should therefore make a strategic decision between a non-directive or combined questioning style.

The non–directive interview is where the interviewee provides a narrative, explanation or an account. It provides the interviewer with information and delivers more protracted answers.

The combined interview **(recommended)** also essentially involves the witness in an open, non-directive interview reinforcing the version of events said with confirmation, either by:

- piggy backing (otherwise known as an echo return), where the information is paraphrased or repeated in the very next question or;
- summary return, when the witness is allowed more freedom to speak but at certain points, the interviewer will provide a summary and ask for confirmation.

An effective interviewer has the skill to shift from one strategy to another; and to take advantage of the related function of each question strategy.

NOTE: It is very rare that the closed question, directive interview "Yes or No" strategy will be used in what is essentially a fact-finding mission at the first interview stage. It usually comes into play, if at all, at the second or third interview of someone who is by that stage a suspect, and even then it is not always used, as it can be an oppressive technique that will simply make the witness less helpful, and possibly render his evidence less reliable. Its most common area of deployment is in the Court Room, in the form of cross-examination or direct examination of a hostile witness.

Interviews and Interrogations - understanding the difference

INTERVIEWS

- to learn about an individual's *perception* and *knowledge* about an event;
- non-confrontational;
- occasions where the investigator will exercise little control; and
- fact-finding exercises.

- include comprehensive document examinations;
- present inquiries into the individual's financial lifestyle;
- are likely to include directive/closed questions, therefore running the risk of revealing what the interviewer already knows;
- do not come naturally for every investigator; and
- will alert the interviewee that he or she is under suspicion.

Interviews (3): The interpretation of body language

Body language has always been more important than spoken language. It is all some species have to communicate with. And it is all ANY species has to communicate with another species. Key "fight or flight" survival decisions have always been made by reference to it. So it is engrained in our instinctive behaviour and perceptions. Sources place body language at between 60% and 80% of the communication traffic that passes between people. It is the core, and primeval, mode of person-to-person communication. Sometimes the communication is so fundamental that it is accepted as being more communicative than verbal communication, designated a "gesture" and not considered to be body language at all, for example, a shrug, but it still is.

Body language is important to the interviewer in two ways. It is not only a guide to the truth or falsity of what is being said by the interviewee, but it is also a way for the interviewer, through control of his or her own body language, to manipulate the messages the interviewee is receiving from the interviewer, and that can be just as important.

To control the interview, the interviewer must learn how to show positive signs and how to create impressions of (i) openness, (ii) authority and (iii) positivity. Don't be body language negative. Learn the "giveaways", and how to avoid them. And remember there is no such thing as body neutral. The body is *always* "broadcasting". A zero result suggests concealment, and is, therefore, a negative. What do you think if you speak to someone and he doesn't reply ? If a more aggressive interview style is needed, there are body language messages that can enhance that adjustment.

Use body language awareness to observe an interviewee. At this stage an interviewer's instincts are important. Body language is the first language people learn to speak, and a powerful instinctive tool. No one needs to be trained in it. All of us are all natural interpreters of other persons' body language. The basis of a "hunch" might just be some body language signs being received. An interviewer listens to gut feelings and instincts.

Cultural awareness

Part of body language awareness involves cultural awareness too. Body language expressions differ between cultures. There are many examples of this, but perhaps the most obvious is in the different form of greetings that exist from the Anglo-Saxon handshake, the French hug and kiss to the Thai "Y" and the Japanese bow.

These are important, but before we examine them, remember what is called "the ultimate gesture", common to all cultures, that is the smile. This is a facial expression, not strictly body language. It is an important way to break down initial communication barriers that may exist in an initial face-to-face meeting.

Also relevant to that first meeting is the handshake, not part of a traditional greeting in Japan, but a significant greeting component in many other cultures. Conversely, the exchange, and reading, of business cards is given more emphasis in oriental cultures. In western culture, although cards are often exchanged, the receivers will usually not pause to read them.

To avoid eye contact in some non-European or US cultures may denote respect to authority. In other western cultures it more likely indicates evasiveness.

The non-verbal signs of "Yes" and "No" vary from culture to culture almost more than any other. It is important to give and receive VERBAL RESPONSES for questions requiring these answers. For example, in Greece and Saudi Arabia, a sudden head-tilt-back movement means "No". In Ethiopia, the same gesture means "Yes". Japanese are very unlikely to express "No" and the sideways head shake may even occasionally mean "Yes". On a related issue, western culture is uncomfortable with silence and may take it as indicating a negative response, while this is not the case in oriental cultures.

The open mouth is not rude in a western society (as in the laugh), but in Japan, for example, it may be and Japanese women cover their teeth when they laugh. That gesture is polite in Japan, but indicates shyness and embarrassment in the West. There again, Western people are uncomfortable with noisy eating, but not so in the East.

The main point about these cultural differences is to encourage awareness of them. An interviewer will not be able to master the full list, but everyone should be alert to the possibility of miscommunication and misunderstanding. That is an important part of manners and courtesy in any event.

A. Body positive

- Standing - still but not stiff or static

stand/sit still for authority. Conversely, fidgeting and jumping about are body negatives. But move "with" the conversation.

- Sitting - open position

legs and arms *uncrossed*

hands on the table - not hidden and, at appropriate moments, palms open (but not upturned: indicates helplessness)

- Standing - feet on the ground

feet apart and flat on the ground. A firm stance and balance.

- Sitting - receptive

either (i) alert, leaning slightly forward or (ii) relaxed, tilting back but not slumped. Facial expressions should be alert. Recognition when listening.

Other non-verbal signs to be aware of

- *Punctuality:* This carries a psychological message. If you are late, it shows a devalued approach to the other person's time. If you are early, you may make the other person feel or appear late. Be neither.
- *Clothes and hair:* not part of body language, but (i) they are part of non-verbal communication and (ii) your awareness that you are well-presented *will* affect your posture and body language. Clean shoes score highly.
- *Face and eyes:* When talking to more than 1 person, pay them all attention. Eye contact should be frequent without staring. Appropriate smiling, but not over familiarity. Alert listening with recognition.
- *Voice delivery:* Audible. Don't rush. Variable tones. No coughs. Don't interrupt.

The "mouth-follows-hands rule"

a) Point. Pause. "You are the guilty man".
b) *Has more impact than:* "You are the guilty man...". Pause. Point.
c) Palms open. "What we need to see..."
d) *Not:* "What we need to see...". Palms open.
e) Beckon, hand open: "Do come in". Not the other way round.

Common phrases that are probably developed with reference to positive body language:

Feet on the ground

Look at you in the eye

Open-handed

Really on the same level

B. Body negative

The Body positive is

- Still but not stiff or static
- Open position: arms and palms
- Feet on the ground
- Receptive and alert

The Body negative is

- Stiff/static
- Closed position: arms and palms
- Feet lifted
- Hostile or inattentive

Other negative signs

Body

- When legs are crossed, the adjacent person that they are crossed away from is receiving a sign of disapproval;
- Un-matched body signs indicate a lack of empathy;
- Fidgeting and moving suggests a lack of authority and/or attention. Feet/hands shuffling indicate impatience or boredom;
- Arms folded across the chest is often seen as defensive, reserved or uninterested in the conversation;
- Standing with hands in pockets suggests a lack of confidence or unease;
- Sitting with legs crossed while shaking one leg or wiggling a foot suggests nervousness or severe discomfort;
- Leaning too far forward indicates aggression; and
- Slouching in the chair suggests you're unprepared or you may be aware you're not up to the task.

Head

- A head tilted to one side is playing the "victim" game, inviting sympathy/rescue;
- As a more extreme example of that is presented by an advocate who, in court, kept his hand at his throat. It was just a mannerism, but he seemed to be strangling himself;
- Jaws clenching and un-clenching indicate anger;
- Yawn: Although usually a sign of drowsiness, yawning in business meetings is actually a sign of mild anxiety or **disagreement**. So when alert listeners yawn, this may signal an opportunity to explore objections or to clarify unvoiced concerns. Yawning is a displacement sign of mild conflict;
- Rubbing the back of your head or neck suggests you're bored by the conversation;
- A fixed unfocused stare indicates attention elsewhere; and
- Clearing throat: nervous.

Can body language spot a liar?

Experts in body language have warned against using body language as a "parlour trick".

The most common claim for body language is that it will reveal a liar. Is this really so?

The claim

Body language:

- The liar will avoid making eye contact;
- Movement restricted;
- Hands touching face, nose, throat or mouth; and
- Body expressions out of synchronization with emotional body/facial expressions.

Other non-verbal signs:

- The liar will often repeat the question in the answer;
- The liar is more likely to be defensive and to justify. The innocent may be aggressive;
- Statements with contractions, e.g. "don't" instead of "do not" are more likely to be truthful. Generally liars' speech and grammar are more formal; and
- Speaking in a higher pitch.

The controversy

- Offensive: One writer says that the liar will be *more* likely to go on the offensive.
- Face Fidgeting: Dr. Samantha Mann, University of Portsmouth, UK has conducted a study which indicated liars touched their noses 20% less than truth tellers[45].
- The point might be that body language, like verbal language, changes over time and is affected by culture. In modern times, the "giveaway" signs of liars have become common knowledge. Now liars seek to override them and the main giveaway may be the lack of signs, as they do so. It is also, perhaps, not to be regarded as an exact science. The general advice is to look for combinations of signs as the presence of more than one of the related signs will reinforce the interpretation impressions.

The conclusion

Body language (like spoken language) evolves. A good example of this is greetings. The most reliable sign on which all currently seem to agree is some limitation of movement.

C. Body neutral

A very short section, because it is suggested that "there is no such thing."

---

45 "The Impact of deception and suspicion on certain hand Movements" Caso, Marichiollo, Bonaiuto, Vrij, Mann - Journal of Non-verbal Behaviour, March 2006 (Issue 30, p1-19).

Really "Body Neutral" is just a subset of "Body Negative". As may be the case with liars, body language may be evolving to develop concealment strategies. With neutral body language, the effect is similar to a person who doesn't reply when talked to – that is in itself innately aggressive (*passive aggressive*), and/or suggestive of avoidance or concealment. Again, however, be culturally aware, and exclude the possibility that it is not fear stopping the person from talking, in which case the investigator/interviewer will need to adopt some of the suggested reassurance strategies.

Remember, the natural healthy human state is ALERT and STABLE, not NEUTRAL. This also applies to body language.

Indeed, "affective flattening" (an unchanged facial expression or expressionlessness) is seen as a "negative" symptom as in, for example, the diagnosis of schizophrenia.

So the "Poker face" may be used to hide a hand, but in a business meeting, there is no such thing. President Mugabe of Zimbabwe is known for his lack of facial expression. There seems little doubt that this is either an avoidance or aggression strategy.

D. Summary

- Learn what body language is, and how it is positioned at the core of all person-to-person non-verbal communications;
- Learn how to maximize a good interviewer's presentation through positive body signs in a business context;
- Avoid the body language "giveaways";
- Develop body language observational skills, and through "body awareness", cultivate the rudimentary skills of body language interpretation; and
- Learn the basic vocabulary of body language, with some famous examples of do's and don'ts.

Interviews (4): Admissions and Conclusions

You need a good start:

- Remember, do not make the investigation personal or take the conduct of the interview personally;
- Expect the deceiver to resist;
- Establish a low-anxiety atmosphere, but project confidence and control;
- Expect an interviewee to withhold and to be uncooperative;
- Do not get into a defensive position;
- Access the interviewee's perspective – Don't have to agree, only understand;
- Prepare some outline of written questions in advance;

- Keep your objective in mind; and
- Begin with easy questions to start a flow of communication. Confirm name, age, and, if possible, home address and job title, etc., as well as the interviewee's years at the firm (to show command of basic facts).

Why do people admit?

- It is the *best action step*
- based upon *what and who is important to them*
- in light of the *information they currently possess*;
- They have two options –co-operation or non-cooperation, admission or denial.
- The choice is theirs.
- Each choice has negative consequences.
- Weighing the alternatives, admission is better than non-admission.

How can you encourage an admission?

- Offer a mutually satisfactory resolution potential.
- Be considerate of emotions and rationalizations.
- Permit the interviewee to maintain his pride.
- Promote compliance.
- Neutralize the fear of consequences.
- Confirm your understanding of his/her concern for the consequences of his/her admission.
- Neutralize the fear of admission,
- Display "I'm OK you're OK" tolerance and compassion. Convey understanding and a readiness to help.
- Discuss the importance of mitigating circumstances for minimizing consequences; and
- Expose the lack of viable alternatives (the smoking gun).

Watch for confident guilt:

- "I am innocent because of my past good acts".
- "I am innocent because of all the fine people that I know".
- "I am innocent because you have treated me so poorly".
- Be attentive to these indications that the interviewee is considering making an admission:
- An interviewee question is a strong sign an admission may be around the corner;
- Incorporate the most appropriate theme to respond to the question asked by the interviewee;
- Reduce the verbal confession to a short concise written statement prepared by the interviewer and signed by the interviewee;
- Prepare it before the confessor leaves;
- Establish within the text the voluntary submission of the confession, approximate dates of the offense, approximate amounts of losses, approximate number of instances and the willingness to co-operate.

When to caution?

In the criminal courts, but not the civil courts, an admission or confession, indeed any witness evidence, is not admissible unless it comes <u>AFTER</u> an actual caution.

The caution is given once the investigator has evidence which would give reasonable grounds for suspecting that an offence has been committed. This is one level of certainty up from the reasonable grounds of belief that was needed to initiate the investigation.

The danger of giving the caution, however, is that the witness will know, as a matter of common knowledge, that the investigation has reached this stage, and may cease to co-operate (as indeed the caution specifically informs he has a right to do so).

Precisely when to give the caution, therefore, is a matter of fine professional judgment, but, we repeat, this does not arise unless it is likely that a criminal prosecution will be brought. Civil evidence is admissible simply if the witness signs the written statement, together with a statement that the evidence contained in it is true.

In both cases, also, there should be no grounds for complaint that the statement was given as a result of any trick or oppression.

The wording of the caution varies from country to country, and is amended over time, so the aspiring investigator is advised to study separately its precise wording. A popular formula in common law jurisdictions including Hong Kong at the time of this writing, is as follows -

> *"You are not obliged to say anything unless you wish to do so but what you do say may be put into writing and given in evidence".*

Many variations of this basic form exist. In the UK, an element is added that warns that the jury may be entitled to draw adverse conclusions from not putting forward a potential defence that you later decide to rely on. Even in Hong Kong, other versions of the caution exist for different circumstances.

Like legal professional privilege, this subject <u>MUST</u> be independently studied by a student investigator, who should obtain CURRENT knowledge of the preferred form of caution for his likely areas of investigation.

Once the caution has been given, the interviewer should review all the evidence given before the caution, and seek its confirmation from the suspect, to ensure that what was said before the caution then becomes admissible in that summary form, assuming the suspect does indeed confirm it.

Conclusion

At the end of the interview, you may think the moment is appropriate to get a signed statement. If you do, take a 10-minute break while you summarize the essential evidence in clear written form and then ask the witness to read, sign and date that statement. If a caution is needed, the statement should include the fact that the interviewee was cautioned. There should also be a verification that the statement is true. The investigator should also record, within the statement, the name and office of the person who took the statement, together with confirmation that it was a statement freely and voluntarily given. A reasonable form of words for establishing these elements at the end might be -

> *"I confirm that this statement is true and that I gave it voluntarily, and not under pressure."*

More often than not, however, the signed statement will come later after you have fully transcribed the evidence, combined from your notes and the tape or video recording. It should still include all of the above elements but will usually then be typewritten and in sequentially numbered paragraphs.

Covert enquiries

It is useful to refer to the sections on monitoring and detection, both overt and covert, in **Chapter 6: Detection**. Further enquiries at this stage may require various forms of covert enquiry, from the basic non-technological surveillance of following or photographing a person, to others. The performance of these tasks is only for a trained investigator and not a subject to be covered here. The investigator's options are to obtain the relevant training, or form a policy to delegate such tasks to outside experts.

Documents

Documents come in paper and electronic form. One is no less a document than the other. They can, and in this area of the law usually *will*, decide the case. It is vital to have strong documentary evidence and to make this a primary focus of enquiry.

Investigators will in particular seek to review, and preserve -

- Correspondence;
- Company memos;
- E-mails;
- Financial record books and files;

- Invoices;
- Orders;
- Receipts;
- Cheques:
- Accounts;
- Reports;
- Log and report books;
- Minutes and agendas of meetings;
- Written procedures and company policies;
- Copies of each person's contract of employment and employment file. These may be confidential and you should ask for written authorization from the person concerned to review them. One of the exemptions under S.58 of the Personal Data (Privacy) Ordinance relating to prevention and detection of crimes may apply so that you do not need to seek permission.
- Petty cash dockets; and
- Where relevant, photographic and video media, including in-house CCTV evidence.

Personal data protection

When an investigator starts to deal with documents it is important to remember the Data Protection Principles. These should be reviewed in full as set out previously in Chapter 6. Three of the most important extracts are set out below, but they need to be understood in the context of the whole scheme as described in Chapter 6.

1. *Schedule 1: Data Protection Principle 3 ("DPP 3") - use of personal data*
    - Personal data shall not, without the prescribed consent of the data subject, be used for any purpose other than-
        - (a) the purpose for which the data were to be used at the time of the collection of the data; or
        - (b) a purpose directly related to the purpose referred to in paragraph (a).

2. *s55 "Relevant Process"*

Section 55 provides for information to be exempted from DPP 3 if it is part of a "relevant process". This includes

- "relevant process" -
- (a) subject to paragraph (b), means any process whereby personal data are considered by one or more persons for the purpose of determining, or enabling there to be determined-.....
    - (i) the suitability, eligibility or qualifications of the data subject for -
        - (A) employment or appointment to office;
        - (B) promotion in employment or office or continuance in employment or office;

- ◦ (C) removal from employment or office; or
- ◦ (D) the awarding of contracts, awards (including academic and professional qualifications), scholarships, honours or other benefits;
- ◦ (ii) whether any contract, award (including academic and professional qualifications), scholarship, honour or benefit relating to the data subject should be continued, modified or cancelled; or
- ◦ (iii) whether any disciplinary action should be taken against the data subject for a breach of the terms of his employment or appointment to office;
  - ◦ (a) whether any disciplinary action should be taken against the data subject for a breach of the terms of his employment or appointment to office;
  - ◦ (b) does not include any such process where no appeal, whether under an Ordinance or otherwise, may be made against any such determination.

3. s58 Crime etc

a) Personal data held for the purposes of -
- ◦ (a) the prevention or detection of crime;
- ◦ (b) the apprehension, prosecution or detention of offenders;
- ◦ (c) the assessment or collection of any tax or duty;
- ◦ (d) the prevention, preclusion or remedying (including punishment) of unlawful or seriously improper conduct, or dishonesty or malpractice, by persons;
- ◦ (e) the prevention or preclusion of significant financial loss arising from-
  - ◦ (i) any imprudent business practices or activities of persons; or
  - ◦ (ii) unlawful or seriously improper conduct, or dishonesty or malpractice, by persons;
- ◦ (f) ascertaining whether the character or activities of the data subject are likely to have a significantly adverse impact on anything -
  - ◦ (i) to which the discharge of statutory functions by the data user relates; or
  - ◦ (ii) which relates to the discharge of functions to which this paragraph applies by virtue of subsection (3); or
- ◦ (g) discharging functions to which this paragraph applies by virtue of subsection (3),are exempt from the provisions of data protection principle 6 and section 18(1) (b) where the application of those provisions to the data would be likely to -
  - ◦ (i) prejudice any of the matters referred to in this subsection; or
  - ◦ (ii) directly or indirectly identify the person who is the source of the data.

b) Personal data are exempt from the provisions of data protection principle 3 in any case in which-
- ◦ (a) the use of the data is for any of the purposes referred to in subsection (1) (and whether or not the data are held for any of those purposes); and
- ◦ (b) the application of those provisions in relation to such use would be likely to prejudice any of the matters referred to in that subsection, and in any proceedings against any person for a contravention of any of those provisions it shall be a defence to show that he had reasonable grounds for believing that failure to so use the data would have been likely to prejudice any of those matters.

For Section 58 it is important to note that although s58(1) reads as if the Data must be "held" for the purpose listed such as the prevention or detention of crime, in s58(2) it is made clear the exemption also applies if the data is merely "used" for that purpose, whether or not it had originally been collected for it. So it is a fairly widely drawn provision, as is Section 55 and the definition of "relevant process".

In all activities with confidential material, the investigator has to remember the principle of proportionality that governs the Data Protection legislation and not to use the material in a disproportionate way, for example, showing it to those who do not need to see it. To be clear, this will be almost everyone except the investigator himself, and would certainly not include other employees. Even when an initial report is made to management, it is unlikely that actual extracts from such material will be used, although the existence of the material may be referred to.

Such deeper disclosure only comes at the later stages, when it is clear an offence has been committed.

Once the evidence has been gathered, it needs to be compiled into a report format that may also be used as evidence in court, if necessary. This will be discussed in the following chapter.

Chapter 9 – Investigation Part 3 - Presentation of evidence, witness statements and reports

Witness Statements: (1) The "narrative" principle

The narrative principle simply requires that evidence be presented in the most logical order, which is presented as it happened, by date and time. At the end of the investigation, the investigator may also prepare a time-line dated chronology of events to reinforce this form of presentation.

Witness Statements: (2) Contents, structure and layout

Witness statements should be written in the first person, with numbered paragraphs and pages, as follows (using the italicized headings) -

Introduction
- Begin with a brief statement of formal details – name, current address, job position, the number of years in that job and any relevant qualifications and experience; and
- Describe the functions and responsibilities of the witness's current job.

Background
- There may be a relevant history or other set of circumstances of which the witness has knowledge that is helpful or puts a certain "angle" on the events that followed. They should go here, as they will have occurred at an earlier stage of the "narrative".

Narrative of events relevant to the matter under investigation
- Once the background is set out, for the remainder of the statement, avoid comment (which can come at the end) and stick to a simple narrative of what the witness knows, setting out the sequence of events just before and after the incident you are investigating. Give dates and time where relevant; and
- Once the whole narrative is told, which will be the bulk of the statement, deal with the final matters.

Comments based on professional knowledge and experience, subject to one important proviso.

- Under a comments section, the witness can insert his opinions and views on any aspect of the incident, as long as those stated are explicitly based on direct or professional knowledge and experience of the matters or people under investigation. Because it is likely that the witness is not an expert witness, as a lay witness, his "expert opinion" will not be admissible. Nevertheless, as a person with first-hand knowledge of relevant matters, the witness has valuable evidence to give from direct observation of events and situations "on the ground". Such comments can still add weight to an analysis and, ultimately, to the proof of a case in court. However, consider this important proviso: such comments and opinions are only of real value if they have been voiced. That makes them, as evidence, a mixture of fact and opinion. For example, "We all thought the accounts procedures were not watertight and we told management so on many occasions," is a mixture of fact and opinion, as is, "We all often talked and wondered about why Mr. X worked late so often, because it never seemed he had done any extra work the next day". Opinions that the witness has kept to himself or herself are less valuable evidentially, but may be included if the investigator considers them important.

Reports (1): The "digestibility" principle

There is nothing worse than walls of figures, reams of stodgy texts, and blindingly dense tables of figures with no clear structure. An investigator's report should be regarded as a technical document, with a clear structure and layout, which is easy to get around, and which explains its own structure.

Key to this digestibility are (i) divisions into sections and subsections, (ii) page and paragraph numbers, and (iii) footnotes containing extra information and cross-references within the document. These should all be tied together with (iv) a list of Contents at the beginning.

Other formal requirements are that the report be signed and dated, stating the investigators' professional office and qualifications.

It is helpful for copies of particularly relevant evidence to be included within the main text as the story is told. The reader will not want to keep cross-referencing and jumping around the document, referring to an Evidence Appendix at the end, or to other areas of the report.

Reports (2): Contents, Structure and Layout

All reports should carry both a **PRIVATE AND CONFIDENTIAL** banner and a **SUBJECT TO LEGAL PROFESSIONAL PRIVILEGE** banner on the front page. In addition, they should carry a specific written Exemption Notice ("health warning") on the first page. An example is included in the model report and is as follows -

IMPORTANT NOTE: This Report is prepared in the context of__(describe the terms of professional engagement, i.e. "a commissioned investigation into a suspected incidence of workplace fraud")__ It is both confidential to and subject to the legal privilege of those persons who have specifically instructed its preparation, and for their eyes only. It is protected from disclosure to any others, in particular either other current or former members, officers, directors or shareholders of __(the client company's name)__, their agents or legal representatives, and the company's special managers or receivers, without specific written authorization.

There are two kinds of reports, preliminary and final.

Preliminary Report:

These are reports made primarily on the basis of an analysis of documents and covert enquiries. The investigation has not yet become public within the firm, and a large part will *never* be known outside the firm. Witnesses have not yet been interviewed.

The following is a list of suggested contents –

Chart 16 – List of sample contents

Contents	
List of Documents in Appendix 1	p.2
Abbreviation Chart	p.3
Section I - Introduction	p.4
Section II - Terms of Reference	p.5
Section III - Overview of Conclusions (Executive Summary)	p.6
Section IV - Analysis of Evidence	p.7
A. Background	p.8
B. The Findings	p.9
C. Supporting Evidence	p.10
D. Supporting Evidence	p.11
E. Potential Interviewees	p.12
F. External Information Sources	p.13
G. Narrative of The Findings	p.14
Section V – Legal Conclusions	p.15
Section VI – Next Steps	p.20

In the Preliminary Report the two key sections, the ones that "give answers", are the Overview of Conclusions (sometimes known as "Executive Summary") at the beginning, and the Next Steps section at the end. These are the two areas on which management will focus. What goes between essentially substantiates the remarks you make in these two key sections.

The Preliminary Report enables the executives of the company to decide what action to take. Fraud being such a sensitive issue, it does not follow that every discovery of fraud leads to a report to the police. If the matter can be settled internally as a disciplinary matter, typically with dismissal and full or substantial asset recovery, large firms, particularly those which are custodians of public money, may choose to not make a report to the authorities, unless they are bound to as a matter of regulatory compliance.

It is important that a preliminary report be as complete as the one that we have attached so that fully informed decisions can be taken by the company.

Final Report:

The Final Report contains less conjecture, and is less discursive and varied in its direction than the Preliminary Report. It should try to present a more decisive style, dealing with the identified fraud now almost as a given, and setting out the evidence which has been collected to prove it. If the decision is taken to move on to the next stage of the investigation, the matter is in the open. Witnesses are interviewed and searches are made of computers and documents throughout the company.

There still may well be confidentialities to maintain however, particularly if the company/organisation is trying NOT to let the matter "go public". The fraud investigator must be extremely tuned-in to this sensitivity.

A good example of a content list of a model report is available in the 2006 Examination Manual of the Association of Certified Fraud Examiners. Other reference sources are available online. It is important to determine whether the company you are preparing the report for has a standard form.

No two fraud reports are the same because (i) no two frauds are the same and (ii) no two fraud investigators are the same. Both are worthy of careful study and comparison. However, each investigator is encouraged to develop his own style.

Reports (3): Pagination, Referencing, Numbering

A final word of caution. The remarks about the importance of pagination, paragraph numbering and the use of footnoted cross-references within the Report(s) are essential to fraud reports. They will be read by busy decision-makers who will require that level of professionalism and "digestibility". In essence, the decision-makers just want the answers, and may well not read the bulk of the report, although, rest assured they will give it to someone else to scrutinize.

Index

www.ingramcontent.com/pod-product-compliance
Lightning Source LLC
Chambersburg PA
CBHW081109220326
41598CB00038B/7292